CONCISE DICTIONARY OF JUDAISM

CONCISE DICTIONARY OF JUDAISM

Edited By

Dagobert D. Runes

PHILOSOPHICAL LIBRARY NEW YORK

Printed in the United States of America

PREFACE

I prepared this small Dictionary upon suggestion of my readers and students. Like all such handbooks, the present one has a practical purpose, namely, to acquaint the casual reader with the meaning of the basic concepts germane to Judaism in its religious, historic and cultural aspects. I have tried to be as concise as possible in my definitions and to make my explanations objectively. In dealing with the great philosophers and theologians of our faith I have endeavored to give the reader more than a listing of the vital data, especially where I felt that those men were of particular significance to our people today. My judgment of the eminence of those treated at length is, naturally, a personal one, and I may therefore have neglected some whom others consider equally important.

I am finishing this little volume in full awareness that it is well-nigh impossible to answer, in such brief space, in full or even at length, all the thousands of questions, issues, and ideas that arise in the study of the so profound and yet so romantic world of Judaism.

I welcome this opportunity to thank Rabbis Maurice J. Bloom, Ben Zion Bokser and Abraham Burstein, for their gracious assistance in reading proofs of this book, and giving me the benefit of their advice.

D. D. R.

CONCISE DICTIONARY OF JUDAISM

A

Aaron (Aharon)

Moses' older brother, born before Egyptian edict of murder for newborn Israelite boys. Guilty of yielding to people in sin of Golden Calf; became first high priest, was denied entrance into Promised Land.

Aaron (ben Mose) ben Asher

(Tiberias, 10th century)

Masorete whose vowels and accents are still used in the Bible.

Aaron ben Elijah of Nicomedia

(Cairo, 1300 – Constantinople, 1369)

Outstanding Karaite theologian and exegete; his *Etz ha-Chayim* was modeled on Maimonides. (W) *Gan Eden, Keter Torah.*

Aaron ben Joseph

(1260-1320)

Karaite philosopher, grammarian, liturgical poet. (W) *Seder Tefilloth, Mibhar.*

Aaron ha-Levi

(Barcelona, 13th-14th centuries)

Wrote much used and translated pedagogic work, *Sefer ha-Chinnuch.*

Abba

(Aramaic, "Father")

Reverential address to sages.

Abba Areka (Rav)

(160-247)

Amora who achieved the authority of a tanna (first and major Talmudic teacher), and who founded the famed Sura academy in Babylonia.

Abbahu

Palestinian amora, 279-320, praised by Roman officials.

Abba Saul

Second-century tanna.

Abbaye

(273-339)

Distinguished Babylonian amora; head of Pumbedita academy.

Abel

(Hevel, "Breath")

Second son of Adam and Eve, slain by envious brother Cain.

Abelard, Peter

(1079-1142)

Catholic philosopher; apologist for Judaism in *Dialogus inter Philosophum Judaeum et Christianum.*

Abimelech

("The father is king")

Son of Gideon, judge of Israel; slew his seventy brothers; cruel ruler of Shechem.

Abin, Rabbi

Third-century B.C.E. amora.

Abiram

A co-conspirator with Korach against Moses; swallowed by the earth.

Abishag

Last love of King David.

Abner

Commander-in-chief for King Saul, his cousin.

Abot

Ethical treatise of Mishnah, known as *Pirke Abot,* Chapters of the Fathers.

Abraham

("Father of a Multitude")

First known as Abram, he was the father of the Jewish people. Came to Canaan from Ur of the

Chaldees; driven by famine to Egypt for a brief time. Put to supreme test of offering his son as sacrifice to God. First to profess monotheism. Made covenant of circumcision. Father of Isaac, and of Ishmael son of Hagar, who became ancestor of the Arab tribes. Buried in Machpelah, cave near Hebron.

Abraham, Testament of

Jewish apocryphal book telling of Abraham's death and ascension to heaven. Probably written in Hebrew in the second century by a Jew or a Jewish Christian.

Abraham Abele ben Chaim ha-Levi

(Gombiner)

Polish Talmudist (1635-1683), who wrote authoritative commentary on ritual law in *Shulchan Arukh, Magen Avraham.*

Abraham ben David of Posquières

(1125-1198)

Known as Rabad III, he opposed the rationalism of Maimonides; wrote many important responsa.

Abrahams, Israel

(England, 1858-1925)

Liberal leader and scholar; editor; author of *Jewish Life in the Middle Ages, Studies in Pharisaism, By-Paths in Hebraic Bookland.*

Abravanel, Isaac

(1437-1508)

A Spanish Sephardic Jew who was in the court of Alfonso V, King of Portugal, but had to flee, at great loss of personal fortune, when a new ruler ascended the throne. From Lisbon he went to the House of Castile, and when the Jews were banished from Spain, he went to Naples, once again in the service of a king, until he was banished by the French rulers. He then fled to Venice where he remained until his death. He was buried in Padua. Abravanel is generally considered the last great Aristotelian. Sometimes a philosophic eclectic, he was principally concerned with the teachings of the

Bible and the modifications of doctrine expounded by the Jews. He was a believer in the Torah and considered the history of the Jews a revelation of God. His studies of the Bible are frequently used as reference by Christian scholars. (W) *Wells of Salvation, The Salvation of the Anointed, Proclaiming Salvation.*

Abravanel, Judah

(Lisbon, c. 1460–Venice, 1530)

Abravanel was one of the outstanding figures of the period of transition between the Middle Ages and the Renaissance. He lived not only at the conjunction of two eras, but also in contact with three cultures—Jewish, Spanish, and Italian. He and his father, Don Isaac Abravanel, fled in 1483 from their native Portugal to Spain, and thence to Italy in 1492. Judah practiced medicine, but he was mainly interested in philosophy, mathematics, and astronomy. For a time he lectured at the Universities in Naples and Rome. The intellectuals of both cities requested his friendship; his was a close association with Pico della Mirandola. During his sojourn in Italy, Judah assumed the name of Leone, the translation of Judah, the Lion. His most famous work, *Dialoghi di Amore (Dialogues about Love)*, was published in Italian, and soon after translated into Hebrew, Latin, French, Spanish, and English. A portion of the book was incorporated in a rabbinical commentary on the Song of Songs. The *Dialogues* are landmarks in the history of aesthetics and of great consequence to the history of metaphysics and ethics. The book promulgates love as a cosmic principle inseparable from being; its spirit, the mirror of reality. The *Dialogues* stressed the spiritual character of physical beauty and helped develop the field of aesthetic idealism. He maintained that true happiness is the "union of the human intellect with the Divine intelligence," and that it is directly connected to aesthetic enjoyment. There is a pantheistic strain in Abravanel's philosophy, but he always emphasized his orthodox Judaism, and tried to reconcile his pantheistic feelings with the Biblical concept of God.

Absalom

("Father of Peace")

Rebellious third son of David. David wept uncontrollably when the handsome young rebel was killed.

Abulafia, Abraham ben Samuel

(1240-1292)

Spanish cabbalist, prolific writer, who attempted to shed all material bonds and to convert the pope, as herald of the Messiah. Arrested, sentenced to death, freed on pope's demise. Had many followers who prepared for return to Holy Land.

Academies

The great talmudic yeshivot, houses of study, were in Palestine and Babylonia; they developed talmudic law and legendry separately. Many presently binding Jewish laws derive from them. Hundreds of talmudic academies have arisen since that time; today they flourish in Israel and large American population centers.

Achad Haam

See GINZBERG, ASHER.

Acharonim

See POSEKIM.

Achdut Ha-avoda

(Poalei Zion)

Zionist socialist party in Israel.

Acosta, Uriel

(1590-1647)

Born in Portugal, the descendant of a Marrano family, religiously observant of Catholicism, the young Acosta prepared himself for the priesthood. But, tortured by doubts about the Christian religion, he decided to flee to Holland. Here he embraced Judaism, not because he was convinced of the truth of his new faith, but he was resolved to deny his former beliefs. He defied Jewish orthodoxy, the very basis of Judaism, because he was incapable of integrating himself into the Jewish community or of understanding its precarious situation and vital needs. His attacks upon the fundamental doctrines of Christianity, which he wrote as a member of the Jewish congregation of Amsterdam, angered the congregation because they felt the Christian authorities who had given the Jews refuge would be offended. Banished, he recanted, revolted anew, was banished anew, and ostracized for seven years. No longer able to endure solitude, he was willing to withstand the most severe penance in order to be allowed to re-enter the Jewish community. But the rigors of the ceremony destroyed his will to survive. Soon thereafter, he committed suicide, unrepenting and irreconcilable. To some extent, he was the victim of his temper, but more so of an era in which it was impossible for an independent thinker to live unharmed outside a religious community. Many novelists and dramatists, Jew and non-Jew, have idealized his life and thoughts, for the poetic transfiguration of his fate is the tragedy of an uprooted man in revolt against tradition and any community based on tradition—the tragedy of a humiliated man, unable to live in isolation whose only alternative was death. He entitled his autobiography *Exemplar Humanae Vitae* (*Example of a Human Life*), but his life was certainly anything but typical.

Adam

The first man and the father of the human race, the name being Biblically derived from the Hebrew *adamah*, "earth," the ultimate substance from which man as a bodily creature is constituted. As the primal source of all human life, Adam symbolizes in Jewish tradition the basic unity and equality of all mankind. Jewish theology treated Adam's fall as a parable of the imperfections which inhere in all human life, but not as their cause. Man is also endowed with an original impulse to virtue; and each person suffers for his own sins.

Adam Kadmon

Aboriginal or primal man,

neither male nor female, closer to Deity than Adam made of dust.

Adams, Hannah

(1755-1832)

American eclectic, who wrote first study of the Jews in America: *History of the Jews from the Destruction of Jerusalem to the Present Time*, Boston, 1812.

Adar

Sixth month of Hebrew calendar: February-March.

Adar Sheni

The second month of Adar, forming Jewish leap year.

Adiabene

Land on the upper Tigris. Queen Helena and her sons adopted Jewish faith during first century.

Adler, Cyrus

(1863-1940)

Conservative leader; first American Ph. D. in Semitics; president of Dropsie College, Jewish Theological Seminary, and many other social and cultural organizations of his people.

Adler, Felix

(1851-1933)

Brought to the United States at the age of six by his father, a rabbi, Felix Adler was also educated for the rabbinical office. He received his doctorate from Heidelberg University and returned to preach at the Temple Emanu-El in New York City. It was here that he failed to refer to God in his sermons. Although he was not disloyal to Judaism, as a rationalist he could not accept the rituals in any literal sense. He left the rabbinate and his friends established a professorship of Hebrew and Oriental literature for him at Cornell University. It was his belief that the principle of the good life can be achieved independently of religious ritual and dogma that led him to found the American Ethical Union and the Society for Ethical Culture in New York. (From there it spread to many groups throughout America and the Continent.) He maintained that the idea of a personal God is unnecessary; that the social and ethical behavior of man, if it makes for harmonious relationships among men, constitutes the Godhead; that man's personality because of its unique and inviolable nature is the central force of the religion. He advocated more than mere religious tolerance: men should reverently respect the religious differences among themselves. In his books *Creed and Deed* (1878) and *Moral Instruction of Children* (1892) he was able to fuse his heterogeneous influences: Judaism, Christianity, Kant, Emerson, and the cogent socialistic ideas of his lifetime. He is noted for his social efforts in such areas as kindergarten and manual training schools, and the abolition of child labor. Other works: *The World Crisis and Its Meaning, An Ethical Philosophy of Life.*

Adon Olam
(Lord of the Universe)

Adoration hymn chanted at opening of morning services.

Adonai

Name of God, meaning "My Lord" or "My Master," used in place of unspoken JHVH.

Adret, Solomon ben
(Rashba, 1235-1310)

Famed Talmudist and thinker of Barcelona, who opposed Maimonides and the early study of philosophy, defended Judaism against attacks by other faiths, and wrote a vast number of legal responsa.

Aelia Capitolina

New name given Jerusalem by Roman Emperor Hadrian (117-138) after breaking the Bar Kokhba revolt.

Afikoman

This word, from the Greek, meaning "after-dish," refers to the last morsel eaten at the seder—half of the central matzah broken off and put away at the beginning of the meal.

Agnon, Samuel Joseph
(1880—–)

Known as Czaczkes in his native Poland, he is a leading fiction writer in Israel, specializing in stories of Chasidim. Best known work *Hachnasath Kallah* (*The Bridal Canopy*).

Agrippa, Julius

(10 B.C.E.-44 C.E.)

Grandson of Herod who governed in Jerusalem 37-44, but was prevented from fortifying the city by the Romans.

Agrippa, Marcus Julius

(28-100)

Son of Julius Agrippa, who favored the Romans and was with Titus at the conquest.

Agudat Israel

Orthodox world organization; party in Israel, with its workers' section, Poale Agudat Israel. Founded in 1912.

Agunah

A woman whose husband had disappeared, and who could not remarry without witnesses to his death. Law opposed by liberal Jews.

Ahab

King of Israel, (c. 873-c. 853 B.C.E.) His wife was Jezebel. He introduced Baal worship, in which the prophet Elijah opposed him.

Ahai of Shabha

(b. Babylon—d. Palestine, 762)

Talmudist who discussed Talmudic law according to portions of the week, in his *Sheeltot.*

Ahasuerus

Name of the legendary Wandering Jew, so condemned for insulting Jesus. This is also the name of the Persian king in the Book of Esther.

Akedah

Binding an animal for sacrifice; specifically, Abraham's binding of Isaac for sacrifice to God—not consummated.

Akiba ben Joseph

(c. 50—c. 132)

One of the greatest of the Palestinian tannaim or early teachers of the Law. The first forty years of his life Akiba spent in complete ignorance; however, at the urging of his wife, Rachel, he devoted himself to the study of the Law and, after twelve years, was recognized as a master. He systematized the accepted Halakhah (religious practice) of his day and propounded new hermeneutic principles which greatly expanded the scope of the Halakhah and facilitated its development. Akiba's genius also made itself felt in philosophy, in Haggadah and in contemporary political events. He, more than anyone else, merits the title, "Father of Rabbinic Judaism."

Akkum

Formed of initials of Ovede Kokhavim u-Mazzalot, those who worship stars and planets; pagans.

Albalag, Isaac ibn

(Spain or France, 13th-14th centuries)

Defender, in his *Tikkun ha-Philosofim*, of twofold truth—revelation and philosophy.

Albo, Joseph

(c. 1380-1444)

Very little is known about the life of Albo, but the few facts that are available present interesting aspects of medieval Jewish life midst Gentile surroundings. Albo was the representative of the Jewish community of Daroca, where the impact and resultant clash of Jewish, Christian, and Islamic thought gave rise to a number of intellectual disputes. He participated in the great controversy at Tortosa (1413-14), where he vigorously defended the Jewish viewpoint of the Talmud. He attained popularity among medieval Jews because of his book *Sefer-Ha-Ikharim* (*Book of Principles*), a defense of Judaism against philosophical criticism and Christianity. Although no new ideas are introduced, the book is important to the general philosophy of religion because it established the criterion whereby the primary fundamental doctrines of Judaism may be distinguished from those of secondary importance. Albo stated that three principles are basic to every revelational religion: a belief in God, the concept of divine revelation, and divine retributive justice.

Alcalde

Minor judicial officer, representing Spanish king.

Al-Charizi, Judah

(1165-1235)

Spanish Hebrew poet, philosopher, traveler; author of *Tachkemoni,* a miscellany in prose and verse.

Alenu

Prayer concluding Jewish prayer services, proclaiming the need of praising God; probably written by Abba Areka.

Aleph (ox)

First letter in Hebrew alphabet.

Aleph-Bet

The Hebrew alphabet: twenty-two letters, all originally consonants, reading right to left; the letters are also used as numerals. In antiquity, as well as generally in modern Israel, the reader supplied the vowels. The Masoretes (traditionalists) after completion of the Talmud, supplied vowel points, preferring marks beneath the letters to the Babylonian choice of supralinear marks.

Alexander of Macedon

the Great (356-323 B.C.E.)

Benevolent conqueror honored in Jewish story; name frequently given Jewish children.

Alexandria

Egyptian port settled by Alexander with Jews. The Jewish population grew to 500,000, and the city became the center of Hellenic culture in Egypt. Ultimately the Jewish community suffered from anti-Semitism and persecution.

Alfasi, Isaac ben Jacob

(1013-1103)

Founder of academy in Spain; writer of responsa and of *Halakhot,* a compendium known as the "Small Talmud."

Alfonsi, Petrus

(1062-1110)

First Moses Sephardi, he accepted Christianity and wrote anti-Jewish dialogues, as well as *Disciplina Clericalis,* compilation of Oriental fables and proverbs.

Al Hamishmar

Organ of Mapam (United Workers Party) in Israel.

Aliyah

Ascent; going up to reading desk in synagogue to partake of Torah reading; journey or migration to Holy Land.

Aljama

Jewish or Moorish quarter, in Sephardic lands.

Alkabetz, Solomon

(1500-1580)

Cabbalist, writer of Sabbath eve song, *Lechah Dodi.* Died in Safed.

Alliance Israélite Universelle

Founded by French Jews in 1860, this international organization seeks to protect and educate Jews suffering from anti-Semitic oppression.

Almemar

(Arabic, "Pulpit")

The fenced dais in the center of a synagogue, often highly ornate, from which the Torah is read forth.

Alphabetic writing

System of writing invented in the second millennium B.C.E. by the Semites or the Egyptians, which greatly improved upon the ideographic and syllabic writings by discriminating between consonantal and vocalic sounds. The Ugaritic alphabet represents a North Syrian attempt, of cuneiform appearance, which was later abandoned. The old Hebrew alphabet, which is probably derived in part from the script of the Serabit-el-Khadim inscriptions (Sinai), is related to the Phoenician and most of the modern alphabets. Square Hebrew, in which the Masoretic text of the Old Testament is written, is an Aramaic transformation of the old Hebrew alphabet.

Alroy, David

False Messiah of twelfth century; murdered by father-in-law, but his followers remained true to his memory.

Altar (Mishbeach)

Elevated structure for sacrificial offerings; made of earth, stone, metal, or metal-covered wood; also used for burning incense.

Amalekites

Arch enemies of Israel; said to stem from Esau.

Amatus (Habib) Lusitanus

(Greece, 1510-1568)

Physician, natural scientist, philosopher, who paved the way for Harvey's discovery of blood circulation.

Amen

("So be it"; "So it is"; "Verily")

Hebrew word of uncertain origin. In the Old Testament the term is used responsively to give solemn ratification to a doxology, to a curse or oath; or to some statement that has been made. In the synagogue (but apparently not in the temple) it was repeated responsively by the congregation after doxologies and following each verse of the priestly benediction. It was not recited after prayers, either public or private, unless these ended with doxologies. Apart from the synagogue usage, individuals were enjoined to repeat it after every doxology, as, for example, those uttered before and after meals. In addition, it might be responsive ratification of any blessing, expressed desire, wish, curse, or oath.

America

Discovered 1492, the very year of the expulsion of the Jews from Spain. The remedy thus was provided at the very time of the affliction; and later America was to become the chief asylum of suffering world Jewry. The United States now has the largest Jewish community in the world; and its sister nations of the Western continents all have their Jewish groups. American efforts and funds, particularly from the United States, have succored persecuted and indigent Jews everywhere, and have today given greatest assistance to the new State of Israel.

American Jewish Committee

Founded 1906 for philanthropic and social educational aid to Jews everywhere, and defense of their rights.

American Jewish Congress

Organized 1917, to aid Jews and Jewish rights, and further Zionist aims. Originator of World Jewish Congress.

American Jewish Joint Distribution Committee

A combination of three fund-gathering organizations, 1914, to provide unified aid to all Jews requiring economic and social rehabilitation.

American Reform

Took final shape at Philadelphia Conference, 1869. Among participants, David Einhorn, Kaufmann Kohler, Isaac Mayer Wise. Basic principles: (1) Rejection of personal Messiah, for common brotherhood of ethical worshiping men. (2) Diaspora not punishment but mission of bringing One God idea to mankind. (3) Rejection of Jewish tribal distinctions (kohanim, etc.). (4) Symbolic interpretation of sacrificial cult. (5) Emphasis on Israel's religious calling. (6) Immortality spiritual, not physical. (7) Without denying the need of cultivating Hebrew, language of ritual and sermon should be vernacular, fully comprehensible to all worshipers.

Am ha-Aretz (Peasantry)

Used by the Talmud and thereafter to mean "ignorant."

Amidah

The "standing" prayer otherwise known as Shemoneh Esre.

Ammon

A nation in eastern Palestine. According to Genesis 19:37-38, the Ammonites were related to the Israelites.

Amnon

Oldest son of David. He seduced his half-sister Tamar, and was killed by her brother Absalom.

Amora

Speaker, interpreter; expounder of Talmudic (Mishnaic) law from compilation of Mishnah to redaction of entire Talmud, in Babylon (where the amoraim were known as Mar or Rav) and in Palestine (where they were designated Rabbi). Their discussions and teachings, 220-550, form the Gemara, lengthier sections of the Talmud that follow each Mishnah.

Amorites

Early inhabitants of Palestine and Syria. They disappeared soon after invasion of Israelites.

Amos

Earliest Old Testament prophetic book, containing poems recited by this Judean shepherd of Tekoa while visiting northern Israel about 750 B.C.E., possibly one long address delivered at Bethel (Morgenstern), but probably excerpts from at least twelve poetic sermons uttered in Samaria, Gilgal, Bethel, etc. In a peak of prosperity, social degeneracy had weakened the moral life until Amos feared Israel would be destroyed by foreign aggressors. He sacrificed his vocation to warn his sister nation, hoping to save her from impending doom by reforming her life. After intense ministry of a few months, he probably was executed following a clash with Priest Amaziah of Bethel. His revolutionary ideas were (1) that Yahweh was a God of Justice, (2) that the Deity expected people to be just with each other, and (3) that worship was a mockery unless accompanied by ethical living. Although still a henotheist, strictly speaking, Amos extended Israel's belief that she was Yahweh's chosen people and paved the way for internationalism and monotheism. He was a literary master, founder of the line of eighth-century prophets, and pioneer in the social gospel.

Amram

Father of Moses.

Amram ben Sheshna

(ninth century)

Head of Sura academy, best known for his prayer book, *Siddur Rav Amram.*

Anan ben David

(eighth century)

Disgruntled founder of opposition sect to rabbinic Judaism, Karaism. He completely ignored Talmud and all post-Biblical legislation and interpretation. Left followers in Egypt and other lands.

Anavah

Humility.

Anaw, Zedekiah

(b. ca. 1227)

Roman rabbi, member of distinguished family, author of *Shibbole ha-Leket* (*Gathered Sheaves*), miscellany of laws and responsa.

Angels

Angels are living creatures of the spirit world, intermediate between gods and men, who may be hostile or friendly toward humanity. Angelology had been specially developed in Persian religion, from which it passed over into Judaism and then into Christianity. In those religions that stressed the personality of the deity, angels served as agents for expressing and revealing the mighty will of God. Judaism had a hierarchy of angels at whose head stood seven (or four) archangels who with their myriads of subordinates discharged various functions. They were servants and messengers of God; their original demonic nature was revealed in their connection with natural phenomena like wind and lightning; they mediated divine revelation and interceded for men before God; and they served as protectors for both individuals and communities.

Aniim Zemirot

"I will chant sweet songs"; Hymn of Glory chanted responsively after Sabbath and festival morning services.

Anshe Knesset Hagedolah

Men of the Great Assembly, organized by Ezra to establish permanent laws.

An-ski, Solomon

(né Rappaport, 1863-1920)

Russian Jewish writer and revolutionary. Author of *The Dybbuk, Between Two Worlds,* and many other works.

Antigonus

(d. circa 37 B.C.E.)

Last of the Hasmonean kings.

Antinomianism

A term meaning Christian opposition to Jewish law, or Jewish opposition to those laws that cannot be rationally explained.

Antiochus Epiphanes

See CHANUKAH.

Antiochus Epiphanes, crisis under

Seleucid king (175-163 B.C.E.), surnamed Epiphanes ("illustrious") and Epimanes ("madman"), who attempted to "coordinate" the Jews in his Hellenization program. Forbade Jewish worship and religious customs under penalty of death and defiled the temple at Jerusalem with an idol 167 B.C.E. His oppression reflected in Dan. 7:8, 25, 8:11-14, 24-26, 9:27, 11:31-36. The temple was purified and rededicated 165 B.C.E. (an event commemorated in the Chanukah festival).

Anti-Semitism

A popular name for the prejudice against Jews, to which various social pressures have contributed. In each period of history, however, this prejudice has found distinct outlets. In ancient times the Jews, like the Christians, were charged with disloyalty to the Roman Empire for refusal to conform to the emperor cults as idolatrous. In the Middle Ages, Jews were condemned for persisting as a religious minority. In modern times anti-Semitism has been fostered by various fascist states which have found Jewish universalism inconsistent with their own tribal nationalism. Anti-Semitism has been condemned by the leading ecclesiastical representatives of both Catholicism and Protestantism. Term first used by German, Wilhelm Marr (1880).

Anusim

Hebrew term for Marranos.

Apikoros

From the Greek "Epikureios" "heretic, agnostic."

Apocalypse

A revelation of mysteries, as in the Book of Daniel.

Apocrypha, Old Testament

(Greek neuter plural of adjective "apokryphos," "hidden, secret")

Writings of scriptural form or content, but excluded from the canon, designated in Hebrew "*sepharim chitzonim,*" "outside books," and *"siphre minim,"* "heretical books" (Sanh. X, 1). The term first bore a laudatory meaning of esoteric writings withheld from the uninitiated because of their sacred and mysterious nature (4 Ezra 14: 44-47; cf. Dan. 12:4,9). Owing to its application to writings of sectarians, like the Gnostics, it has acquired (since the second century) a disparaging sense of noncanonical, untrustworthy, spurious, and even false and heretical. It came to denote especially works of doubtful origin or authorship, pseudepigrapha. Specifically, the Apocrypha of the Old Testament contains fourteen books commonly found in Greek Bibles (the Septuagint) and the Latin Vulgate in excess over the Hebrew Bible. They are (in the order in which they appear in the Authorized and in the Revised Versions): (1) 1 Esdras; (2) 2 Esdras (same as 4 Ezra); (3) Tobit; (5) Additions to Esther; (6) Wisdom of Solomon; (7) Ecclesiasticus or Wisdom of Jesus the Son of Sirach; (8) Baruch, with the Epistle of Jeremiah; (9) Song of the Three Children; (10) History of Susannah; (11) Bel and the Dragon; (12) Prayer of Manasses; (13)

1 Maccabees; (14) 2 Maccabees. Excepting 1 and 2 Esdras and the Prayer of Manasses, these books form part of the Catholic canon. At the council of Trent (1546) their canonicity was formally reaffirmed. The Protestants, on the other hand, following Jerome, excluded them from sacred Scriptures. Accordingly they initiated the usage of Apocrypha for a collection of books appended to the Old Testament and (up to 1827) generally added to every English Bible. While some Reformed Churches banished the Apocrypha from public worship, the Church of England prescribes its reading in public services "for example of life and instruction of manners." Catholics class these books as "deuterocanonical" and reserve the name Apocrypha for other quasi-scriptural books in excess over those of the Vulgate to which Protestants give the name Pseudepigrapha. The difference in nomenclature is purely arbitrary. The term Apocrypha may be well applied to the whole body of noncanonical literature of the Jews produced in the last centuries B.C.E. and the first century C.E. in Palestine and in Egypt, mostly in Hebrew and Aramaic and some in Greek. The books of the Apocrypha proper may be classified as: (1) historical, including histories, historical tales, legends, supplements, and embellishments of the Old Testament; (2) didactic or sapiential; and (3) apocalyptic. The last type predominates in the Pseudepigrapha. The entire material is of greatest value for the Jewish religious development between the Old and the New Testaments.

Apologetics

Defenses of Judaism (or any faith) against attack. Great Defenders of Judaism began with Philo and Josephus. Judah Halevi's *Kuzari* upheld the Jewish faith. There were famous treatises by Profiat Duran, returned after forced conversion, *Al Tehi Ka-Avotecha* (*Be Not Like Your Fathers*); and Isaac Troki, *Chizzuk Emunah* (*Strengthening Faith*). Seventeenth century, Manasseh ben Israel; eighteenth, Moses Mendelssohn.

Apostate

(Greek, "standing off")

Medieval renegades from Judaism often became its bitter enemies (cf. Johann Pfefferkorn, 1500). However, some nineteenth-century defectors became self-critical (Heine), and even helpful to Jewry (Disraeli). European Jewry has lost many of its weak, ambitious, or professionally or socially self-seeking members to the dominant faith.

Apostle

(Greek, "Messenger"; Hebrew, "Shaliach")

Referring, in the Hellenic and Roman eras of Palestine, to collectors of religious taxes and donations.

Aram

A people of Shem descent, north and east of Canaan; related to Hebrews. Greeks called them Syrians.

Aramaic

Sister tongue of Hebrew, also called Chaldaic. Became common language of Middle East, for business, daily activities, even diplomacy. Spoken by Jews during Babylonian captivity and on their return. Most of the Talmud, parts of the Bible, certain prayers, are in Aramaic. Bible translations into Aramaic are called Targumim.

Arameans

Ancient people kindred to the Hebrews, who occupied mainly the region of Syria. Often mentioned in the Old Testament.

Arba Ammot

The Four Ells considered each man's personal domain, for ritual and legal transactions.

Arba Kanfot (Four Corners)

A four-cornered garment with opening for head, bearing the fringes ordained by Bible law (TZITZIT). Worn under regular clothing as substitute for prayer shawl, and constant reminder of Jewish ethical commands.

Arba Kosot

The four cups of wine ordained for each attendant at Passover seder.

Arbaah Minim

Four species—the lulav, etrog, myrtle branches and willow, combined for ceremonial use on Sukkoth.

Aristobulus

(3rd or 2nd century B.C.E.)

Alexandrian Jewish philosopher, who visioned Judaism as source of Greek philosophy and literature. Another Aristobulus was a Hasmonean king in second and first centuries B.C.E.

Aristotle

(384-322 B.C.E.)

The great Greek philosopher whose ideas influenced Abraham ibn Daud, Maimonides, Spinoza, and many other Jewish thinkers.

Ark

The large craft built by Noah to preserve all earth creatures and save them from the flood sent upon a sinning world.

Ark of the Covenant

A portable, gold-decked wooden sanctuary carried by the Israelites on their wanderings. Two golden cherubim with outspread wings symbolized the presence among His people of their divine King. Within the Ark rested the stone tables inscribed with God's covenant. Placed in the Temple of Jerusalem; its ultimate history is not known.

Ark of the Law

Receptacle in which Torah scrolls are kept in the synagogue, generally in wall niche.

Arlosoroff, Chaim

(Ukraine, 1899-Tel Aviv, 1933)

Labor leader and politician in Palestine, murdered by political opponents; active in socialist Hapoel Hatzair.

Armageddon

Plain of Esdraelon, where many battles were fought; hence New Testament depiction as place for decisive battle between good and evil. Probably from Hebrew "Har Megiddo."

Aron ha-Kodesh (Holy Ark)

Decorated wall closet in synagogue containing Torah scrolls.

Artaxerxes I

Emperor of Babylonia, 465-425 B.C.E. During his reign, Judaism was revived in that empire.

Aryan

Sanskrit "noble-born." But word refers to language rather than to persons.

Asch, Sholem

(1880-1957)

Yiddish novelist and dramatist, Poland and the United States. His depictions of Jewish life are masterful; in his latter years he created controversy by his predilection for Christological themes and apologia (THE NAZARENE, MARY, THE APOSTLE).

Aseh; Lo Taaseh

Positive and negative commands.

Aseret Yeme Teshuvah

The Ten Days of Penitence, from Rosh ha-Shanah through Yom Kippur.

Ashamnu

Confession of sin, Yom Kippur. Also recited daily.

Asher

One of Jacob's sons; his tribe occupied coastal strip north of Carmel.

Asher ben Jechiel

(Germany, 1250–Spain, 1327)

Greatest authority on Jewish law of his time; wrote responsa, commentaries, and a collection of halakhot up to his time called PISKE HA-ROSH (he was called Rosh for Rabbi Asher) or HA-ASHERI.

Ashi bar Simai

(352-427)

Reviver and head of the academy of Sura, Babylonia; chief editor of the Babylonian Talmud, and last accepted authority among amoraim.

Ashkenaz

Bible reference to unknown northern tribe. The name was later given to the Germans; and the Jews of that country, of France, and the north of Europe were called Ashkenazim, as distinguished from Spanish and south European Jews, called Sephardim.

Ashkenazi

Term mainly applied to Jews of northern and eastern Europe. Origin not clear (Genesis 10:3; Jeremiah 51:27).

Ashmedai

King of the demons.

Ashtoreth

(Possibly a distortion of Ashtart, on the analogy of "bosheth," "shame"; Gr. Astarte)

Supreme goddess of Canaan and female counterpart of Baal (cf. Baal), known in Babylonia as Ishtar and in South Arabia as Athtar (masc.). Ever virginal, she was also the fruitful mother and creatress of life. The Philistines seem to have emphasized her warlike character (I Sam. 31:10). The numerous Ashtaroth represent various forms under which she was worshiped in different places (Judges 10:6; cf. I Kings 11:13). Her name was given to the city of Og, king of Bashan (Deuter. 1:4).

Asseret ha-Dibrot

Ten Commandments (Words).

Assimilation

The constant process of attrition whereby Jews have been swallowed up, or have consciously permitted themselves to be swallowed up, by their environment. At all times there have existed self-hating Jews called assimilationists.

Assumption of Moses, The

A fragment of a larger apocalyptic work now lost. Its form is that of an address delivered by Moses to Joshua before his death. It was originally written either in Hebrew or Aramaic, and was composed during the first decade after the death of Herod, or about 6 C.E.

Athaliah

Usurping queen of Judah, 843-837 B.C.E.; overthrown by the priests.

Atonement, Day of

(Yom Kippur)

The holiest day in the Jewish year, observed as a fast from the evening of the ninth of Tishri to that of the tenth, essentially expiatory and characterized as "a Sabbath of solemn rest" and "a holy convocation," upon which all manner of work is forbidden under the threat of excision (Lev. 23:27-32). The ceremonial of the day at the Temple centered in the person of the High Priest and his atoning sacrifices and confessions (Lev. 16. Cf. Mishnah Yoma). Following the fall of the Temple, a liturgy of prayer replaced the priestly ceremonial, stressing confession of sin, repentance, and wholehearted reconciliation with God and man. Cf. Kol Nidre.

Atzeret

Conclusion; used for concluding observance of festival; word derived from "gathering" or "detention," original meanings. Shemini Atzeret is concluding day of Sukkoth; Atzeret is Talmudic term for Shavuoth, conclusion of Omer count.

Auschwitz-Birkenau

Where four million Jews were gassed and burned by the Nazis in Polish extermination camp. Later transformed by Polish government into museum, displaying mountain of victims' hair for stuffing mattresses, children's toys taken from them before the final agony, wooden legs, artificial teeth, and other articles—all carefully catalogued by the systematic German brain.

Auto-da-fé

("Act of Faith")

A euphemism employed by

Spanish inquisitors, and their likes, for burning infidels.

Av

Eleventh month of Jewish year.

Av Bet Din

Father of the Court–judicial president in Talmudic era, and later.

Av ha-Rachamim

("Father of Mercy")

Ancient prayer still recited for martyred Jews. Recited in many congregations only on Sabbaths preceding Shavuoth and Tishah B'Av.

Avel

Mourner (after the burial).

Avele Zion

Mourners of Zion–a category which includes most Jews of history; specifically, a premedieval sect of lamenters in Jerusalem.

Avicebron

See IBN GABIROL.

Avinu Malkenu

("Our Father, our King")

Invocatory phrase, used in a series of prayers during the Days of Awe.

Avodah

Service–specifically, the sacrificial Temple service as performed by high priest; today, referring to Yom Kippur observance and other synagogue rituals. Chasidic concept of life dedicated to God.

Avon

Sin through weakness.

Ayin Ha-ra

"Evil eye" superstition troubling Jews since Talmudic times; the superstitious have employed prayer slips, amulets, sacred herbs, and other means to contravene its effect. They use Yiddish expression, "*Keineinhara,*" ("No evil eye!")

Azarah

Court of synagogue, Sephardic.

Azariah (Help of God)

A king of Judah; and one of the men in the furnace with Daniel.

Azazel

Meaning unknown; Talmud thus denotes the mountain on which scapegoat is sent, to carry people's sins into the wilderness, on Yom Kippur.

Azharot ("Admonitions")

Liturgical songs on the 613 divine commands of the Torah.

Azriel

(1160-1238)

Spanish author of cabbalistic works.

Azulai, Chaim Joseph David

(Jerusalem, 1724–Livorno, 1806)

Prolific traveler and writer in all branches of Jewish lore; bibliographer of rabbinical literature; author of SHEM HA-GEDOLIM, dictionary of literary history.

Azut panim

Boldface; one who is impudent or insolent.

B

Baal (ruler, lord)

Name of local gods, often symbolized as bulls, and worshiped with frenzy and lewdness.

Baal Shem-Tov

(1700-1760)

After seven years of solitary meditation, Israel ben Eliezer began to teach, in 1740, a mysticism which later became known as Chasidism. This earned him the title of Baal Shem-Tov (Master of the Good Name), even though in his early years he had been despised by his people as an ignorant and inefficient man. He taught that the divine spirit is omnipresent in each man and in everything that exists. Therefore, it is possible to serve God in even the most trifling of actions. In contradistinction to other schools of mysticism and to various Jewish mystical doctrines, he declared that the pleasures of the senses are not sinful, because man must serve God with his body as well as with his soul. In his teachings, all things, including the lowest acts, had dignity. Although he did not reject learning, he put prayer above scholarship, insisting that his followers pray "with gladness" and forget, through religious concentration, all the sufferings imposed by life. The teachings of Baal Shem-Tov gained a large number of adherents among the Jews of Eastern

Europe, who at that time were subject to frequent persecutions and whose economic situation was constantly growing worse. These people were impressed by his kind and humble personality and revered him as a saint. He received gifts of immense value, but ended each day by distributing all his wealth among the poor. He saved many coreligionists from despair, enabled them to endure extreme hardship, and imbued them with the spirit of confident piety.

Baal Tefillah

Leader of prayer service.

Baal Tekiah (Tokea)

The functionary who sounds the shofar on the high holidays.

Baba Book

A long popular Yiddish version of a medieval romance; also called BABA-MAASEH—a term applied to any fantastic story.

Babel

The capital of Babylonia, in which empire the authentic Talmud was created. This is also the name of the Tower of Babel, building of which was halted by a confusion of tongues. From Babylonia Abraham began his pilgrimages. It was the place of the great captivity, 586-538 B.C.E. The great Jewish academies were in Nehardea, Sura, and Pumbedita.

Babel, Isaak

(b. 1894)

Russian Jewish fiction writer of twentieth century. Died in a Soviet concentration camp.

Babylonian Captivity, The

The Babylonian Captivity refers to the period in Jewish history beginning with the year 597 B.C.E., when the first large group of Judeans, together with their king Jehoiachin or Jeconiah, were deported by Nebuchadnezzar to Babylonia, and ending in the year 538 B.C.E., when Cyrus, conqueror of Babylonia, issued a rescript granting the Jews the right to return to Jerusalem and rebuild the Temple. During this period several other deportations took place, among them that following destruction of the Temple in 587 B.C.E. The sources differ as to the number of Jews who were carried off to Babylonia (cf. II Kings 24:14, 16; Jeremiah 52:28-30), however, it is safe to assume that at least 20,000 were deported. The condition of the Jews who settled in Babylonia was comparatively favorable. The soil was much more fertile than that of Judea and easily supported many Jewish farmers. Some Jews even rose to positions of wealth. So comfortable was the lot of the Jews that many refused to take advantage of the proclamation of Cyrus, but contented themselves instead with giving financial aid to those who were returning to Jerusalem. Approximately 42,000 Jews returned to Judea in 538 B.C.E. Those who remained in Babylonia formed the nucleus of the community that, centuries later, was to become the center of Jewish learning and culture.

Badchan

Jesting, singing master of ceremonies at a Jewish wedding.

Baeck, Leo

(1873-1956)

Liberal German rabbi who stood up against Hitler; author of theological works.

Baer, Dob

(Volhynia, 1710—Anapoli, 1772)

Known as the Great Maggid, or the Maggid of Meseritz, this Chasidic leader succeeded Baal Shem-Tov. His teachings produced open split between Chasidim and their opponents, the Mithnaggedim, led by the Vilna Gaon. His maxims were published posthumously by his disciples. (W) *Maggid Debarav Le-Yaakov.*

Bahir

Oldest of classical cabbalistic works, first known in Provence, eleventh century.

Bahya ibn Pakuda

(c. 1050)

Little is known of the personal life of Bahya, except that he was a *dayyan* (judge at the rabbinical court) in Saragossa toward the end of the eleventh century. His book, HOBOT HA-LEBABOT (*The Duties of the Heart*), expressed his personal feelings more elaborately than was usual for the Middle Ages. It depicted the noble, humble soul and pure, imperturbable mind of a man ever-grateful to God, motivated by his love of God. Bahya regarded the soul elevated toward God and liberated from the shackles of earthly existence as evidence of purification, communion with God as the ultimate goal. However, his teachings neither imply nor result in neo-Platonic ecstasy. He remained faithful to the Bible and the Talmud. Unlike many other schools of mysticism, he differentiated between man and God. Although a religious moralist, he resolutely subordinated moral righteousness and lawful action to the pious contemplation of God, for the latter served as the most effective control of egoistic instincts and passions.

Balaam

Prophet "not of the people" who came to curse Israel, but, in view of its splendor, blessed Israel instead.

Balfour Declaration

Letter of November, 1917 to Lord Rothschild from the British Secretary of Foreign Affairs, supporting creation of a Jewish national home in Palestine.

Balkis

Queen of Sheba who visited King Solomon.

Bar Giora, Simon

A general who defended Jerusalem in the Roman war against the Jews (66-70). Led in chains by Titus through Rome and then executed.

Bar-Ilan University

Youngest university in Israel, at Ramat-Gan, near Tel Aviv, motivated and supported by religious Zionist funds.

Bar Kokhba

(Aramaic, "son of a star")

Leader of a Jewish revolt (132-135) against Hadrian. Name, originally Bar Koziba, was changed to Bar Kokhba on his assumption of command. His generalship prolonged a brave but futile fight against Rome. He died in the Battle of Bethar, 135; otherwise little is known about him.

Bar Mitzvah

(bar, "son"; mitzvah, "duty or command")

Term applied to (1) a Jewish boy on attaining his thirteenth year, the age of religious duty and responsibility; (2) the solemnization of the event by calling up the boy, on the following Sabbath, as one of the seven men for the reading of the weekly portion of the Law, or, as the eighth man, to read the Haphtarah (prophetic lesson). Occasionally the boy delivers a religious address. The event is celebrated by the family. Henceforth the boy is included among the ten males required for public worship, and wears phylacteries during weekday morning prayers. Non-orthodox synagogues have a Bat Mitzvah ceremony for girls.

Baraita

Any teaching of the tannaim, Talmudic teachers, "external" to the Mishnah. One of any such collection, called Baraitot.

Barak (Lightning)

General under Deborah; defeated Sisera.

Barash, Asher

(Galicia, 1889–Tel Aviv, 1952)

Hebrew poet, essayist, fictionist, editor.

Barrios, Daniel Levi (Miguel) de

(Spain, 1626–Amsterdam, 1701)

A Marrano who ultimately became an orthodox mystic; historian and prolific poet. Traveled extensively; for a while was follower of Shabbetai Zevi.

Baruch

The companion and amanuensis of Jeremiah (Jer. 36:4-32). "Baruch" is likewise the title of four different, noncanonical, Jewish books, of varying character, all ascribed to or centering about the figure of the historical Baruch. These writings date in all likelihood from the first and second centuries C.E.

Basar b'chalav

Meat in milk. It is forbidden to mix meat and dairy foods, or their dishes and utensils.

Bashan

Biblical name for north Transjordania.

Basilea, Solomon Abiad

(1680-1743)

Mantuan cabbalist, commentator, yeshivah head.

Basle Program

Adopted at first Zionist Congress (1897), proclaiming general scope of the movement aiming at establishment of a publicly and legally secured homeland for the Jews.

Bass, Shabbatai ben Joseph

(1641-1718)

Much traveled Polish Jew who founded Hebrew bibliography.

Bat Kol

Meaning "Daughter of a Voice," this phrase refers to a reverberating prophetic utterance from heaven. The angel Gabriel was generally credited with these pronouncements, which were not decisive in legal matters.

Bat Mitzvah

Modern counterpart of Bar Mitzvah, for girls.

Bathia

Egyptian princess who saved the infant Moses.

Bathsheba

Widow of Uriah, sent to battle death by King David; she became David's favored wife and mother of Solomon.

Batlan

An "idler," whose freedom

from ordinary labors often permitted him to engage in prayer and study at the synagogue.

Beard

Anciently the beard and mustache were considered ornamental symbols of manhood. Because the Bible prohibited cutting the corners of the beard (Lev. 19:27; 21:5), most Jews in the past let it grow entire. But removal by chemicals or electric razor does not violate the Biblical law; and most observant Jews of the current generation do not wear beards.

Bechorot

Talmudic treatise on first-born in man and animal.

Bedersi, Jedaiah

(d. 1340)

Hebrew poet in south France; wrote midrashim and a lengthy poem, BECHINAT OLAM (*Test of the World*).

Bedikat Chametz

Search for leaven before Passover.

Beer-Hofmann, Richard

(1866-1945)

Austrian novelist, poet, dramatist, who expressed his love of Judaism in his works.

Beer-sheba

"Well of the Oath" or "Seven Wells"—key city in Israel's northern Negev; in Bible most southerly Palestinian city opposing Dan, in north.

Beilis, Mendel

Central figure in ritual murder trial, 1913; ultimately exonerated (Kiev).

Bekavod

Dignified.

Belfer

Yiddish for "Behelfer." Assistant to Hebrew teacher.

Belmonte, Jacob Israel

(Madeira, 1570-Amsterdam, 1629)

Poet; a founder of Amsterdam Jewish community.

Belsen

German extermination camp. See Auschwitz.

Belshazzar

(6th century B.C.E.)

Last king of Babylonian Empire; it was his end prophesied in wall writing: "*Mene, mene, tekel upharsin.*"

Bemidbar

("In the wilderness")

Numbers, fourth book of Pentateuch.

Ben

"Son of"; Aramaic, "*bar.*"

Ben Adam Lachavero

Duties of man to man.

Ben Adam Leatzmo

Duties of man to himself.

Ben-Avigdor (A. L. Shalkovitch)

(1866-1921)

East European writer and publisher of Hebrew books.

Ben-Gurion, David

(Plonsk, 1886—)

Labor Zionist leader who became first premier of the Republic of Israel; chief architect of the new state.

Ben-Yehudah, Eliezer (Perelman)

(Lithuania, 1858-Jerusalem, 1922)

Teacher and writer who did most to revive Hebrew; author of great DICTIONARY OF THE HEBREW LANGUAGE.

Ben-Zvi, Isaac

Born 1884 in Poltawa, this historian and Hebraic scholar is second president of Israel.

Benedictions

Hebrew "*berachot,*" from the word meaning to kneel. They are recited in the liturgy and on all occasions when thanks are given to God. Hebrew benedictions begin, "*Baruch Atta Adonai,*" "Blessed art Thou, O Lord." Blessings of the Oneness of the Lord and His infinite attributes are the spiritual thread running through all Hebrew religious literature and liturgy.

Beni Israel

Groups of Jews in India, dark and probably mixed with Hindu blood.

Benjamin

Youngest son of Jacob by Rachel; one of the tribes of Israel.

Benjamin of Tudela

Twelfth-century traveler who described Jewish communities on Mediterranean and Indian Ocean; wrote MASSAOT SHEL RABBI BINYAMIN (*Travels of Rabbi Benjamin*).

Berachyah

(c. 12th or 13th century)

The literary fame of Berachyah is chiefly founded upon his MISHLE SHUALIM (*Fox Fables*). Some of these were of his own invention; others were derived from the fables of Aesop, the Talmud, and the Hindus, but even in the adaptation of plots to his own Hebrew style, he displayed poetic originality and narrative talents. The best-known of his philosophical works, encyclopedic in quality, is SEFER HAHIBBUR (*The Book of Compilation*). Here, he developed the ideas of Saadia, Bahya Ibn Pakuda, and Solomon Ibn Gabirol. He was versed in the eastern and western branches of Jewish philosophy, and was well acquainted with medieval French and English literature. The personal life of Berachyah is solely conjecture. He was called Berachyah Ben Natronai Hanakdan. His father's name indicates descent from the Jewish scholars of Babylonia, which may help to explain Berachyah's knowledge of Hindu stories. His surname means "punctuator," probably an allusion to his profession of scribe or grammarian. There is no agreement as to the time, place, or country in which he lived. Some of his biographers assume that he wrote during the twelfth century; others during the thirteenth century. Some maintain that he lived in Provence; others in northern France, and still others in England. It is not improbable that he was an itinerant teacher, scholar, and writer.

Berakhah (Benediction)

Basic form of prayer, praise, thanksgiving in Jewish faith. See PRAYER.

Berek, Joselovicz

(1763-1809)

Leader of Polish Legion that fought for Napoleon; fell in battle against Austria.

Bereshit

Genesis.

Bergelson, David

(Ukraine, 1884-1952)

Important Yiddish novelist and short story writer, executed by Stalin.

Bergmann, Hugo

(Prague, 1883—)

Philosopher who taught at Hebrew University.

Bergson, Henri

(1859-1941)

Brilliant French Jew, one of the most notable and influential philosophers of contemporary times. He did not clearly declare the religious implications of his philosophy until the appearance of his last work. He arrived at a modified, non-scholastic theistic position, moving away from the absolute, static perfection of scholastic theology toward a God who is manifest in concrete events and in the intimate history of living individuals and organisms. He plainly rejected the absolute deity of Aristotle for a dynamic personal God of love, the a priori method for an empirical approach. Bergson was a temporalist theist, conceiving of God not as complete but as growing in knowledge, goodness, spiritual power, and social awareness. As the self-identity of progress, God is that which alters and in altering remains Himself. Being the subject of change, He endures and escapes the ravages of time. The vital impetus is God operative in evolution and present in all life and reaching a higher level of attainment of His purposes in man. The reality of time, the waste in the onward movement of the vital impetus, the importance of freedom, novelty, and struggle, connect God with the thought of a limited, but ever creative, cosmic force. Social processes, customs, mores, and taboos, strengthened by religious beliefs and practice, in preventing man from using his newly acquired intellectual power or reason for individual ends detrimental to society, are the first, conservative influence of the two sources of morality and religion. Later on in social evolution the weight of custom is liable to hold mankind back, by its inertia and rigor, by lack of deep inward emotion and aspirations, threatening freedom and making progress impossible. This is averted by a second, higher and intuitive source of morality and religion. Despite theological differences among the great mystics, all basically agree in testifying that they have come into contact with a deeper spiritual reality than the majority of men. While only a few are capable of such profound inward experience, most individuals have felt something sufficiently approximating it and react sympathetically to the testimony of these souls. They follow to some extent their leadership. Bergson believed religion and morality can further spiritual, social, political, and economic progress. Regarding human personal immortality as probable, he hoped psychic research would ultimately demonstrate it scientifically. (W) *Creative Evolution, Time and Free Will, Matter and Memory.*

Berr, Isaac

(1744-1828)

Champion of Jewish emancipation in France.

Bertinoro, Obadiah

(15th cent. C.E.)

Rabbi and halakhic authority in Italy and Palestine; chief work, COMMENTARY ON THE MISHNAH.

Beruriah
Heroic wife of the famed tanna, Meir (second century).

Besamim
Spices. Used at Havdalah, outgoing of Sabbath service, in decorative containers, to allay regrets at passing of the holy day.

Besht
See BAAL SHEM-TOV.

Bet Am
House of the People; synagogue.

Bet Din
("House of Judgment [Law]")
Jewish court, employing religious and Talmudic law.

Bet ha-Knesset
("House of Assembly")
Synagogue.

Bet ha-Midrash
("House of Study")
Another name for the synagogue, in which Jewish lore was regularly studied.

Bet ha-Mikdash
House of Sanctity; synagogue.

Bethlehem
Bet Lechem—House of Bread; home city of David.

Bezalel
Biblical artist who carved the Tabernacle.

Bialik, Hayyim Nahman
(1872-1934)
Outstanding Hebrew poet. Born in Russia, died in Israel, where he was leader of cultural life and shaper of Zionism. The poet of both the vanishing ghetto and the new nationalism. In Israel, wrote stories, fairy tales and essays, and last great poem, YATMUT. Also collected legends of the Talmud and Midrash in SEFER HA'AGADA. Hebrew novels: ARYEH BAAL GUF, ME-ACHORE HA-GEDER.

Bibago, Abraham
(d. Spain, 1489)
Philosopher, commentator, religious disputant; author of DEREKH EMUNAH (*Way of Faith*).

Bible, the

The word is derived from "biblia," plural of the Greek noun "biblion," meaning "book." That in turn was derived from the word for Egyptian papyrus, the writing material on which books were written. The word was mistaken by Latin readers as the feminine singular. Hence we have a singular noun for what is really a library of 66 books. Thirty-nine books comprise the Old Testament.

I. Pentateuch (Chumash):
1. Genesis
2. Exodus
3. Leviticus
4. Numbers
5. Deuteronomy

II. Prophets (Neviim):
6. Joshua
7. Judges
8. Samuel I
9. Samuel II
10. Kings I
11. Kings II
12. Isaiah
13. Jeremiah
14. Ezekiel
15. Hosea
16. Joel
17. Amos
18. Obadiah
19. Jonah
20. Micah
21. Nahum
22. Habakkuk
23. Zephaniah
24. Haggai
25. Zechariah
26. Malachi

III. Writings (Ketuvim):
27. Psalms
28. Proverbs
29. Job
30. Song of Songs
31. Ruth
32. Lamentations
33. Ecclesiastes
34. Esther
35. Daniel
36. Ezra
37. Nehemiah
38. Chronicles I
39. Chronicles II

The rabbis count only 24 books —combining Samuel, Kings, the twelve minor prophets, Ezra, Nehemiah, and Chronicles.

Biblical Age (longevity)

That of Moses, 120 years; this

number has served as good wish toward others.

Bikkur Cholim

Visiting the sick—a pious duty, carried out in the past by Chevra Kadisha.

Bikkurim

First fruits; discussed in Talmudic tractate.

Bilbul

Confusion.

Bilu

Name of Russian student group who founded Rishon le-Zion and other settlements in Palestine in 1882 and thereafter. The name is made of the initial letters of *Bet Yaakov lechu venelcha,* "House of Jacob, come ye and let us go."

Bimah

Reader's stand in synagogue.

Birkat ha-Mazon

Benediction over food; grace after meals.

Birnbaum, Nathan

(1864-1937)

Austrian writer who was a forerunner of political Zionism. (W) *Self-Emancipation, National Rebirth.*

Biro-Bidjan

Siberian province on the Amur, turned over to the Jews in 1928 by the Soviets, apparently as a means of stifling Russian Zionism. The project proved a complete failure, leaving the few Jews remaining in poverty and a minority among Tartars and other anti-Semites. There was a synagogue there, but no rabbi.

Birth control

Rabbinic law prohibits birth suppression, but does not reject use of contraceptives after two or three children are born.

Bishop of the Jews

Title of Jewish convert in medieval Germany.

Biur (Exposition)

Bible commentary of Mendelssohn and his followers.

Blessing of New Moon

Special prayers at synagogue on previous Sabbath; and outdoors at moonrise.

Bloch, Ernest

(b. Geneva, 1880—–)

Called the "Isaiah of music," this liturgical composer has had a profound effect upon his disciples.

Blood

Drinking or any use of blood is prohibited under penalty of death (Lev. 47:10); reply to those who accuse Jews of using human blood.

Blood Accusation

The charge repeatedly rising in Europe since the Crusades that Jews use Christian blood for Passover purposes. Some confessions were gained through torture. Dark Ages trials on ritual murder charges were conducted in Russia and Germany as late as 1911 (Beilis) and 1929 (Memel).

Bloomgarden, Solomon

See YEHOASH.

Bnai Akiba

Orthodox youth organization.

Bnai Brith

Fraternal order founded in New York 1843, now international; institutes and aids welfare movements; Anti-Defamation League; Hillel Foundation (colleges and universities).

Boerne, Karl Ludwig

(Frankfurt, 1786–Paris, 1837)

Physician and journalist who showed regret over his conversion by becoming a powerful defender of the Jews. (W) *Letters from Paris.*

Boethusians

Sadducee sect which opposed the Pharisees on the validity of the Oral Law and life in the hereafter; they disappeared during the revolt against Rome in the year 66.

Book burning

Frequent practice of Christian Europe; greatest Jewish book burning took place under Hitler.

Bostanai ben Chaninai

(618-670)

First Babylonian exilarch.

Brafman, Jacob

(1825-1879)

Renegade who furthered Russian anti-Semitism in nineteenth century with fraudulent pamphlets "unmasking" Jewish "plans to conquer the world." See PROTOCOLS OF THE WISE MEN OF ZION.

Brainin, Reuben

(1862-1939)

Russian-born U.S. Hebrew literary critic.

Brandeis, Louis Dembitz

(1856-1941)

Notable as a Justice of the United States Supreme Court Brandeis was a juridical heretic, who had the satisfaction of seeing his views acknowledged by orthodox jurists. Many of his dissenting opinions have since become the law of the land. He was greatly inspired by Oliver Wendell Holmes, Jr., a colleague of his on the Supreme Court bench, and he subsequently had great influence over his former teacher. Both of them stressed the historical development of law, the necessity of adapting legislation to the dynamic economic and social changes, and the social and broad cultural responsibilities of jurists and legislators. Both frequently dissented from the majority Court opinion. Brandeis was opposed to socialism and claimed it did not increase industrial efficiency. He was favorably inclined toward labor, small businessmen, and cooperative enterprises. Although he protested that he had no general philosophy and thought only within the context of the facts that came before him, he was not only a philosopher of law, but also a social and political philosopher. His views never lost their vital contact with the facts of daily life. He distrusted those whose reasoning bounded far ahead of the facts, and considered those thinkers inadequate whose lack of imagination did not enable their ideas to withstand the test of experience and subsequent events. He always treated opponents fairly when they indicated a willingness to compromise. He firmly believed in the ultimate possibility of reconciling the varied interests of individuals, in overcoming the antagonism between the individual and society and in espousing a basic loyalty to one's fellow man and to the community. He hoped that a humanistic education would culminate in the realization of his ideas.

Brandeis University

Waltham, Mass., is the home of the university named after the late Justice.

Brandstaedter, Mordecai David

(1844-1928)

Humorous depicter, in Hebrew prose and verse, of Galician Chasidim.

Brenner, Joseph Chaim

(1881-1921)

Born in Ukraine, this novelist, journalist, dramatist, soldier was killed by the Arabs in a Palestinian pogrom. Givot Brenner is named after him. (W) *One Year.*

Bridal Fast

Except on Sabbath and festivals, bride and groom are traditionally ordered to fast during the day until their wedding is completed.

Brit Milah

Covenant of Circumcision, commonly termed bris. First practiced by Abraham; all later Jews have removed sons' foreskins on eighth day after birth, with naming and blessings for the future.

Brith Trumpeldor

Revisionist-Zionist organization.

Brod, Max

(Prague 1884-19 ?)

Novelist who moved to Israel; major novel, REUBENI, KING OF THE JEWS. Also writer on religion, Zionism, socialism.

Brody

Galician town important in Jewish events; center of Haskalah, eighteenth and nineteenth centuries.

Bruch, Max

(1838-1920)

Composer of widely employed Kol Nidre liturgical music.

Brunschvicg, Léon

(1869-1944)

French Spinozist.

Buber, Martin

(b. 1878—)

Martin Buber is one of the leading exponents of Chasidic philosophy. His grandfather, Solomon Buber, was the Chasidic scholar who provided impetus to the mystical movement, and the revival of some of the early tenets and practices of Judaism that resulted in a cultural renaissance among the eighteenth century Jews of Eastern Europe. Martin Buber, a student of the mystical religions of China and India, as well as that of medieval Christianity, maintains that the Judaic experience of divine immanence, as it is expressed in the Talmud and realized in prayer, has a unique importance for all peoples. He accepts the mystical concept of man's communion with God. Religious redemption is the central theme of his spirituality. He believes that the philosophies of religion and sociology have made for greater human cohesiveness. (W) ON THE SPIRIT OF JUDAISM, TALKS ON JUDAISM, THE KINGDOM OF GOD.

Buchenwald

German extermination camp. See AUSCHWITZ.

Budko, Joseph

(Poland, 1888-1940)

Principal of Bezalel School in Israel; noted illustrator.

Bund

Social Jewish workers' union. Founded in Wilna 1897; supported Yiddish as Jewish national language.

Burial

Although there was some warrant for cremation in ancient Judaism, burial in the earth is the norm among Jews. Interment in a mausoleum is permitted, if it bears no symbols of other faiths. Early burial is enjoined by Jewish law.

Burla, Judah

(1886—–)

Jerusalem novelist of life of Oriental Jews.

C

Cabbalah (tradition, heritage)

Devotional literature inspired by a mystical immediacy between God and man. God reaches man through a chain of ten immaterial forces, emanations or manifestations called Sefiroth. These emanations make physical life possible on earth, through the participation of the Lord. Great classic of Cabbalah literature is the Zohar (*q.v.*). The Sefiroth are Kether (Crown). Chokhmah (Wisdom), Binah (Intelligence), Chesed (Mercy), Geburah (Judicial Power), Tifereth (Beauty), Netzach (Victory), Hod (Glory), Yesod (Foundation), and Malchuth (Kingdom). Among important early works on the Cabbalah are SHIUR KOMAH—on measurement of God's dimensions: and SEFER YETZIRAH (*Book of Creation*).

Cabbalists, Christian

Pico della Mirandola—translated cabbalistic works into Latin. John Reuchlin—author of cabbalistic theses, DE VERBO MIRIFICO, and DE ARTE CABBALISTICA, about 1500. Paracelsus, greatest physician of medieval Europe, and also student of Cabbalah.

Cadaver

Handling of dead body renders handler unclean. Food of animals otherwise permitted cannot be eaten if they die naturally.

Caesarea

Seat of Roman governors in Palestine.

Cain

Oldest son of Adam, doomed to bear a sign on his forehead for murdering his brother Abel; himself later killed by Lamech.

Calendar

(Luach, "table")

Jewish year began in spring in Bible times; present arrangement stems from thirteenth century. Hillel II (359) issued rules for uniform calendar. Israelites returning from Babylon brought back names of months still in use. Year is 354 days of 12 months of 29 or 30 days; seven out of nineteen are leap years, with 13 months (Adar and Second Adar).

Calle

Jewish quarter, Sephardic.

Canaan (lowland)

The "Promised Land" conquered by Joshua and settled by nine and a half of the twelve tribes of Israel, the others occupying territories East of the Jordan River. The term later was employed to include all Palestine west of the Jordan.

Candle lighting

Before Sabbath and festivals. The Sabbath blessing is: "Blessed art Thou, O Lord, ruler of the universe, who hath sanctified us with His commandments and commanded us to kindle the light of the Sabbath."

Capa rotunda

Cloak prescribed for Jews; Sephardic.

Capistrano, Johann von

(1386-1456)

Franciscan monk, virulent Jew hater, responsible for burning of Jews in Breslau.

Capsali, Moses

(1420-1495)

First chief rabbi of Turkey; an ascetic scion of a distinguished family.

Cardozo, Benjamin Nathan

(1870-1938)

It has been said of Justice Cardozo, that "by the magic of his pen, he transmuted law into justice." He was one of the greatest American philosophers of law; chief judge of the Supreme Court of the State of New York, for more than ten years; Justice of the Supreme Court of the United States.

Caro, Joseph

(Toledo, 1488–Safed, 1575)

Author of Standard Jewish Code, SHULCHAN ARUKH (*Prepared Table*), Venice 1564. This contains ORACH CHAIM (*Way of Life*), on daily duties, Sabbaths and festivals; YOREH DEAH (*Teach Understanding*), *rituals*; EVEN HA-EZER (Stone of Help), family law; CHOSHEN MISHPAT (Shield of *Righteousness*), civil law. The SHULCHAN ARUKH is derived from Caro's large codex of the Halakhah, BET JOSEPH (*House of Joseph*).

Caucasian Jews

Of legendary origin, but traceable to ninth century.

Central Conference of American Rabbis

Organization of Reform rabbis, founded 1889 in Detroit by Isaac M. Wise.

Chabad

Word formed of initials of cabbalistic sephiroth, Chochmah, Binah, Daat (wisdom, reason, intuition).

Chabib, Jacob ben Solomon ibn

Spanish Talmudist, 1460-1516, who compiled and annotated Haggadic portions of Babylonian Talmud, calling his work EN YAACOB.

Chad Gadya (One Kid)

Aramaic folksong ending Passover Haggadah; like "The house that Jack built."

Chagall, Marc

(Russia, 1887––)

Modern painter, with predilection for Jewish subjects.

Chajes, Zvi Hirsch

(1805-1855)

Talmudic scholar who helped found Jewish science in Galicia; wrote important INTRODUCTION TO THE TALMUD.

Chakham

Sage.

Chaldea (Kasdim)

Southern Babylonia.

Chalilah

"Perish the thought."

Chalitzah

This Biblical ceremony, to absolve a man of marrying his childless brother's widow, means "removal." The widow removes his shoe and publicly spits upon the recalcitrant. See YEBAMAH; Deut. 25.

Challah

White braided Sabbath bread; name of the dough tithed from bread baking.

Chalukah

"Distribution" of funds collected for the poor in Palestine —custom traceable to thousand years of fund-gathering for academies and rabbis in the Holy Land.

Chalutz (Pioneer)

Vanguard of youthful settlers in Palestine.

Chamberlain, Houston Stewart

(1855-1927)

British son-in-law of Richard Wagner, whose writings inspired Nazi race theories.

Chametz

Food prepared with leaven, by extension referring to all foods and utensils forbidden on Passover.

Chamishah Asar bi-Shevat

Fifteenth day of Shevat—Jewish Arbor Day.

Chananeel ben Chushiel

Rabbi in Kairwan, Tunis,

lived 990-1050, who wrote commentaries on Bible and Talmud.

Chanukah (Hannukah, Dedication)

Festival commemorating defeat of Syrian Greeks by Maccabees, 165 B.C.E., and rededication of desecrated Temple in Jerusalem. Not mentioned in Bible, but in Apocrypha. Eight days, beginning Kislev 25. Judas Maccabeus won over Antiochus IV (Epiphanes), who had massacred 40,000 Jews in Jerusalem alone (169). Celebrating miracle of tiny cruse of pure oil found in Temple burning for eight days, one candle is lit on first night, increasing to the left each evening of eight-day festival; a shammash (beadle) candle lights then from left to right. Blessings and Psalms are recited. Maoz Tzur ("Oh Fortress, Rock of my salvation") is sung. Children receive gifts and play a tops game (dreidel). A half-holiday, like Purim.

Charoset (clay-like)

See SEDER

Chas veshalom

"Peace, forbid it!"

Chasdai ibn Shaprut

(915-990?)

Physician to Caliph of Cordova; scholar who wrote EVEN BOCHAN (*Teststone*), dialogue between Hebrew and Christian; best known for his correspondence with King Joseph of the Chazars, converts to Judaism.

Chasidim (Chasid, "pious")

The party of the pious, the devout champions of the Law and upholders of the traditional faith, who flourished in Palestine during the second and third centuries B.C.E. From their circle came the most determined opposition to the worldly and assimilationist Hellenizers among the people. They were the backbone of the Maccabean revolt and forerunners of the Pharisees.

Chasidism

A significant and extensive mystic movement which rapidly spread among the Jews of Poland in the second half of the

18th century. It came in the wake of earlier mystic messianic movements and the social and economic collapse of the Jewish communities of Eastern Europe following the Cossack uprisings in the middle of the 17th century. The Chasidic movement spread very rapidly, and by the middle of the 19th century, it embraced nearly one-half the Jews of Eastern Europe. The movement stressed the values of piety, spiritual exaltation, and the joy of complete surrender to God, as a counterpoise to rigid religious formalism, rabbinic intellectualism, and the spiritual depression of the times. "Pure faith without any sophistries" was the keynote. The essence of Judaism was the love of God, and the way to God was open to the poor and ignorant man whose prayer is sincere and whose faith is boundless, as to the scholar steeped in Talmudic lore or to the ascetic who denies himself the innocent enjoyments of life. The theologic emphasis was upon the omnipresence of God, man's ready communion with Him, and the power of fervid and ecstatic prayer. The movement, steeped in religious emotionalism, came into violent conflict with official orthodox Rabbinism centered in Lithuania, seat of great rabbinic academies, and its followers were frequently persecuted and excommunicated by their opponents, who were known as Mithnaggedim. The Chasidim came to have their own separate synagogues and special prayerbooks and their own communal organization within the larger Jewish community. For a time Chasidim and Mithnaggedim would not intermarry. The founder of this movement was a man of humble origin, Israel ben Eliezer (d. 1760) who, because of his reputation as a healer and a miracle-worker, was known as Baal Shem-Tov (*Besht,* "Master of the Good Name"). The movement was always centered in the personality of a tzaddik (the righteous one, also called rebbi) who was the supreme guide of his disciples and their mediator before God. These tzaddikim came to exercise enormous influence over their followers, some of them establishing hereditary dynasties, holding "court" and accumulating great wealth. The movement began to decline sharply toward the middle of the 19th century as a result of its own inner stagnation and the spread of modernism and secularism among the Jewish masses. Among the more prominent leaders of the movement were Rabbi Baer of Meseritz (d. 1772), the successor to Besht; Rabbi Jacob Joseph of Polonnoye (d. 1782), first literary figure in Chasidism; Rabbi Nahum Tchermobyl (d. 1797); Rabbi Levi Isaac of Berdychev (1740-1809); Rabbi Shneur Zalman of Liady (1746-1819), philosopher and rationalist of the movement and founder of the "Habad," a branch; and Rabbi Nachman of Bratzlav (1770-1811).

Chatan Bereshit

"Bridegroom of Genesis," honored with first reading of the Law on Simchat Torah.

Chatan Torah

"Bridegroom of the Law," who is honored with final reading from the Pentateuch on Simchat Torah.

Chatat

Sin offering in Temple.

Chaver

Associate, colleague; scholar; member of religious group observing all Levitical laws.

Chazak

"Be strong"—a greeting or an exclamation when a book of the Bible is concluded.

Chazakah

Method employed by Jewish law to possess and retain property.

Chazars

Tatar tribe in the Crimea who became converts to Judaism under their King Bulan, about 750. Conquered by Christian Russians, eleventh century. See JUDAH HALEVI.

Chazir

Swine.

Chazzan

Originally superintendent of education, crier, sexton, conductor of services; now cantor only.

Cheder (Room)

Elementary Hebrew school.

Chelev

Intestinal fat or tallow prohibited for consumption by Jewish dietary laws. Punishment of KARET (being cut off) named in the Torah.

Cherem (Ban)

Excommunication from the Jewish community. There is a brief ban—Niddui—which permits the immediate family of the culprit to speak to him. Offenses range from heresy to criminal libel and treason. A general cherem can be proclaimed against certain practices, as the interdiction against polygamy by Rabbi Gershom ben Judah in the eleventh century. Famous cases of the invoking of the cherem include those of Spinoza, Uriel Acosta, and Shabbetai Zevi.

Cherethites and Pelethites

Philistine tribes, who formed bodyguard for David.

Cherub, cherubim

(Hebrew, kerub, kerubim)

Winged celestial beings, part human and part animal, who served as the chariot of the Almighty and as guardian angels. Figures of cherubim decorated the doors and the walls of the Temple of Solomon. Two cherubim made of olive wood, and covered with gold, were set up in the inner Sanctuary of the Temple, their overarching wings touching each other in the middle of the chamber beneath which rested the Ark. The Ark itself had two cherubim of gold set up, facing each other, at the two ends of the Ark-cover (Kaporet), their wings spread out on high. It was here, between these two cherubim, that the Deity revealed Himself and communicated His commands (Ex. 25:17-22; Num. 7.89). Yahweh is therefore referred to in the Bible as "He Who is enthroned upon the cherubim" (I Sam.

4:4; II Sam. 6:2; II K. 19:15; Ps. 80:2, 99:1). There were no cherubim in the Second Temple. In the vision of Ezekiel (Chaps. 1 and 10) the Divine Throne rested upon the wings of four cherubim, each of which had the form of a man with four faces—those of a man, a lion, an ox, and an eagle—and each possessed four wings, under which were the hands of a man. The soles of their feet were calves' soles. Each cherub had a wheel at its side which moved as the cherub moved, and both cherub and wheel were full of eyes. These cherubim served as the divine chariot. Cherubim were the guardian spirits not only of the Sanctuary and the Ark, but also of the Tree of Life after the Fall (Gen. 3:24). In the angelic hierarchy developed in later times, the cherubim came to be variously placed in the scale, but their function remained primarily that of guardian angels. Such subsidiary deities of composite forms acting as winged guardians, one finds in Babylonian, Assyrian, Hittite, and Egyptian mythology, and representations of them are to be seen on monuments and sculpture. It has been suggested that the cherubim were the personifications of clouds, wind, or storm.

Cherut

"Freedom" Party in Israel, formed by Revisionists.

Cheshvan

Second month of Jewish year.

Chet

Sin of error or negligence.

Chevra Kadisha

Holy (Burial) Society.

Chibbat Zion (Love of Zion)

This organization, whose members were known as chovave (lovers) of Zion, was a precursor of the Zionist movement.

Chiddush

"New" exposition of the Talmudic text.

(by Michelangelo, 1516)

PLATE 1. The Prophet Moses

PLATE 2. Hebrew Captive in Egypt.
Stone Relief, 13th Century B.C.E.

FROM THE DEAD SEA SCROLLS

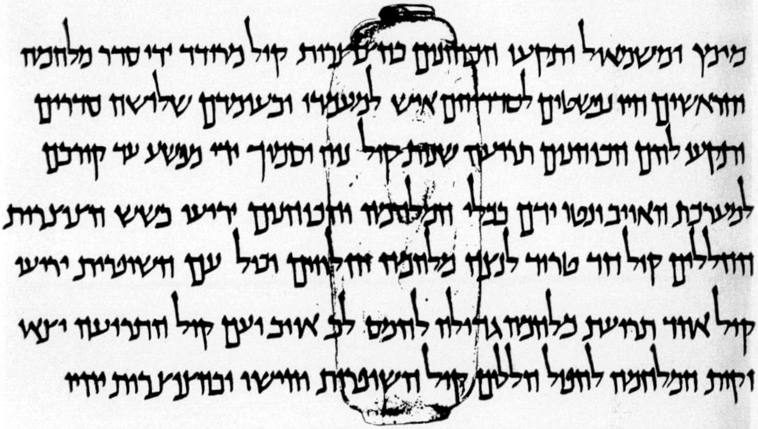

FACSIMILE OF PART OF "THE WAR OF THE SONS OF LIGHT AND THE SONS OF DARKNESS"

(*Courtesy Rina Gallery, Jerusalem. Israel Office of Information*)

PLATE 3.

(*Collection of Albert Keller, New York*) Rembrandt

PLATE 4. King David

(© *Matson Photo Service*)

PLATE 5. Graves of the Judges (Sanhedrin) near Jerusalem

PLATE 6. The "Wailing Wall." Foundations of Herod's Temple

PLATE 7. Philo Judaeus (c. 25 B.C.E.–c. 50 C.E.)

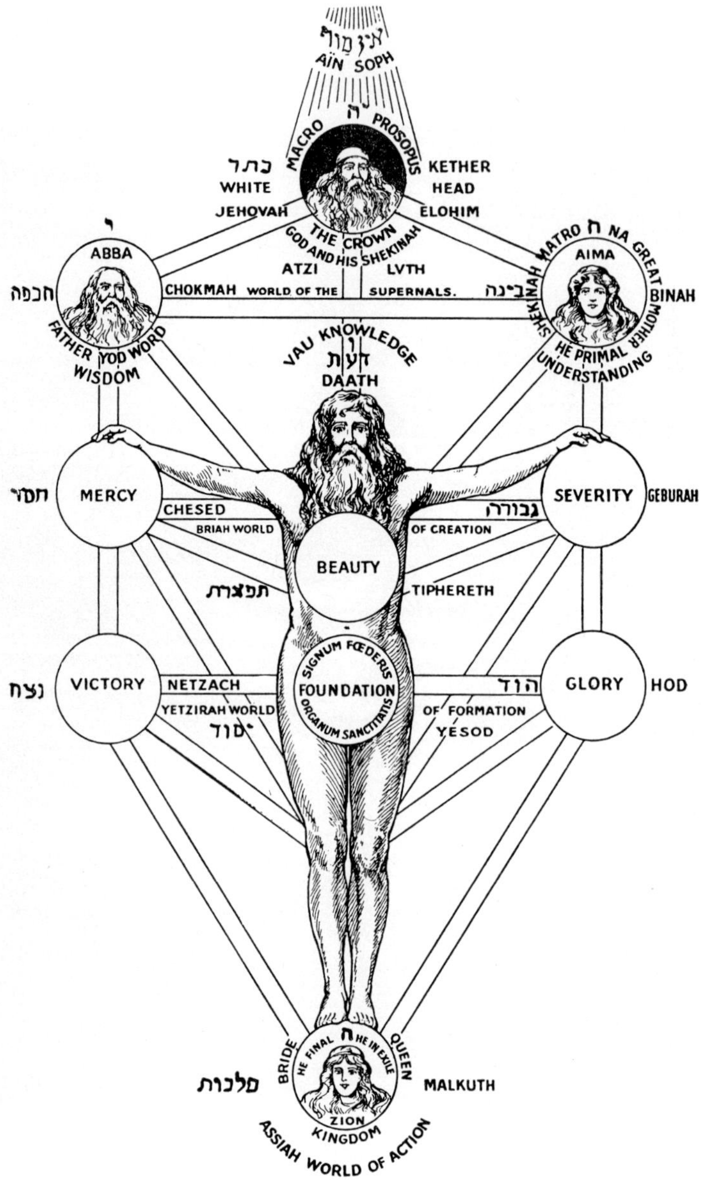

THE SACRED TREE OF THE SEPHIROTH

PLATE 8.

(Caballah)

PLATE 9. Clifford's Tower at York in 1807

This tower was built in 1068 and was the scene of the massacre of the entire local Jewish population in the year 1190.

PLATE 10. Crusaders Massacring Jews

Ich bin ain Buchlinn
der Juden veindt ist mein namen
Ir schalckhait sag ich vnnd wil mich des nit schamenn
Die lang zeyt verborgen gewest ist als ich thůn bedeütenn
Das wil ich yetz offenbarn allen Cristen leüten
Dann ich bin mit yren hebraischen schrifften wol bwart
Vnd dem verkerten geschlecht die warhait nit gespart

Jesus nazaren⁹ rex iudeoꝝ

יהושע נזרות ומלך היהודים

yehoschua nazeros vmelech haiehudim

PLATE 11. Title Page of the Renegade Pfefferkorn's Anti-Jewish Book (1509).

PLATE 12. Title Page of Luther's Anti-Semitic Pamphlet

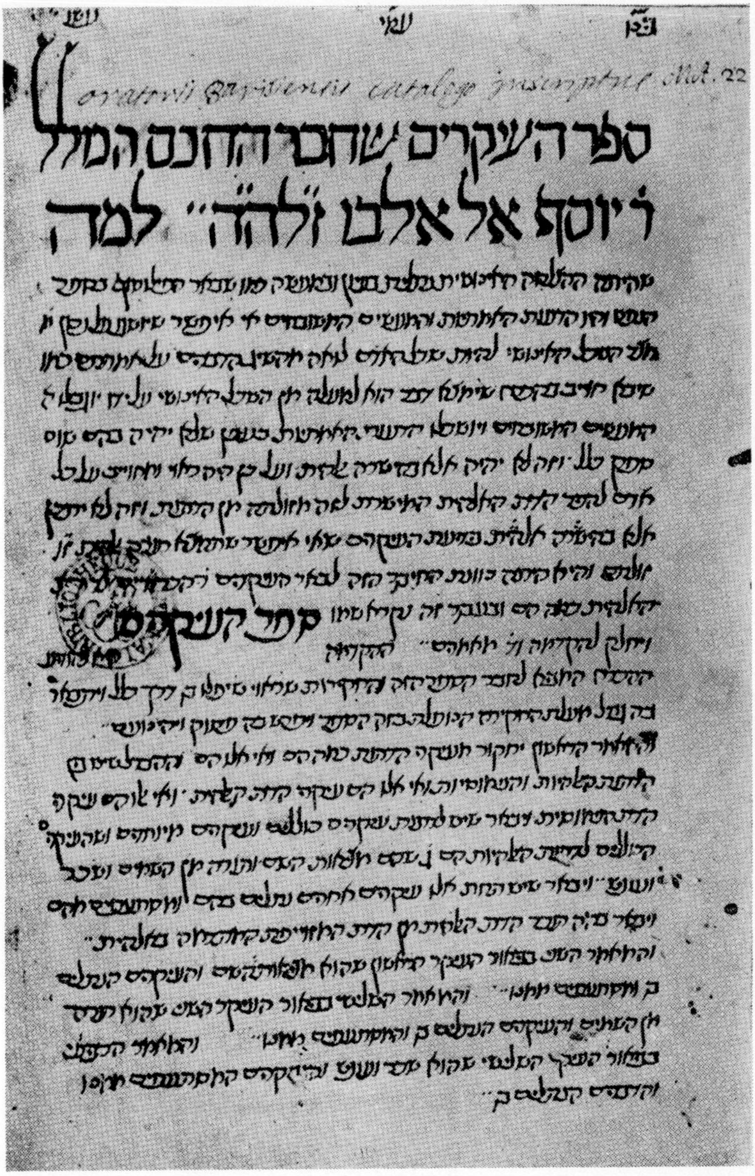

ספר העקרים שחבר החכם המל
ר׳ יוסף אלאלבו זלה״ה למה

PLATE 13. *Sefer-Ha-Ikkarim* by Joseph Albo

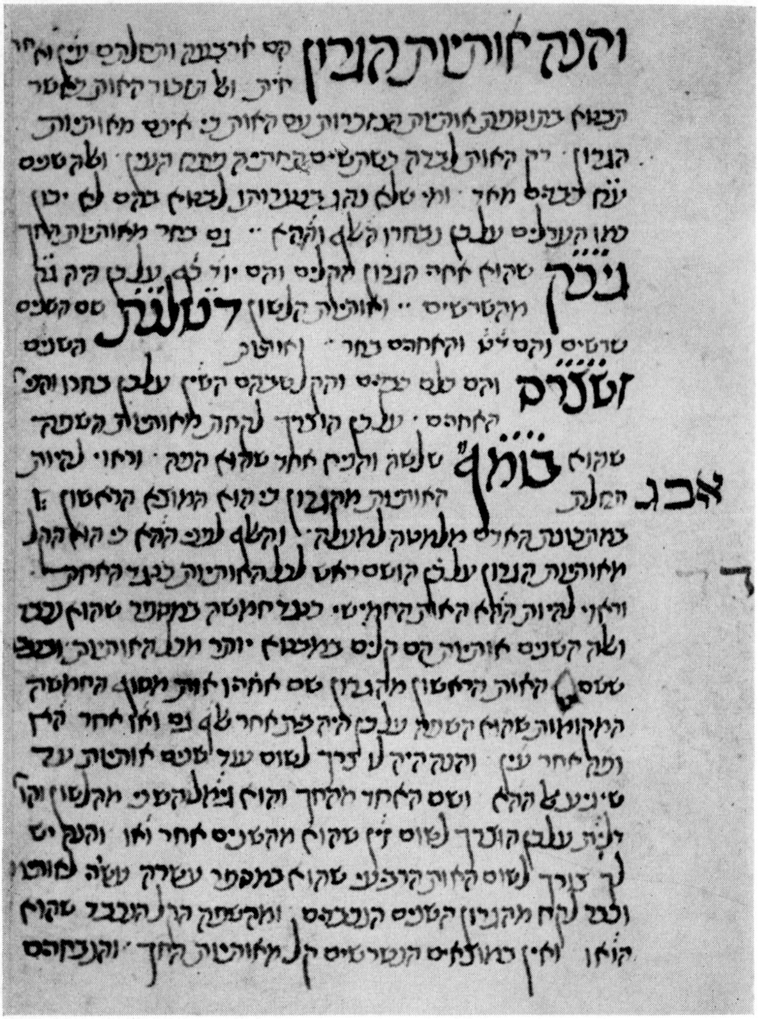

(*Courtesy of Frank J. Darmstaedter*)

PLATE 14. Manuscript by Abraham ibn Ezra

Grammatical Excursus—Introduction to Commentary on Book of Exodus

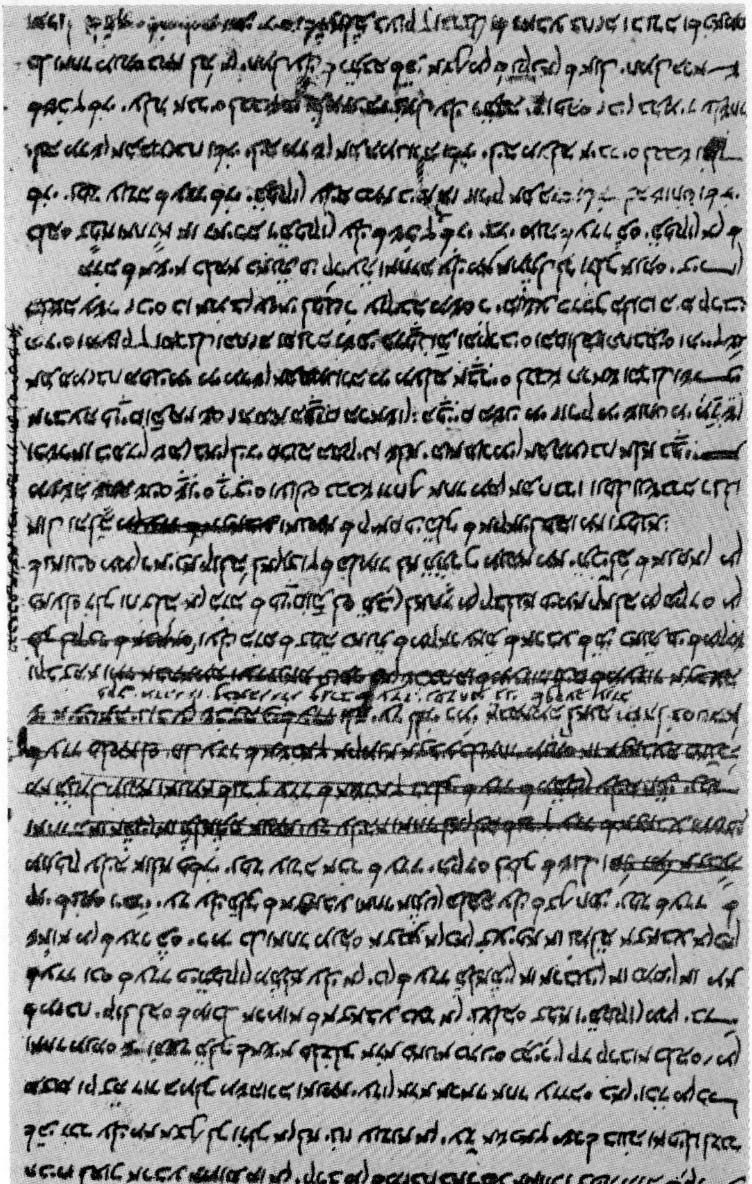

(*Courtesy of the* "Israelitisches Familienblatt," *Berlin*)

PLATE 15. Autograph from Maimonides' *Perush Hamishnajoth*

PLATE 16. *Maimonides* (1135-1204)

Child naming

Since the Hasmoneans, it has been customary to name a Jewish child after a deceased relative. In early Middle Ages use of generic terms (Emunah—"Faith") and Christian names became common. Hence two names proved necessary—the religious name (shem ha-kodesh), used in all rituals, and a civic designation (kinnui).

Chillul Ha-Shem

Desecration of the Divine Name.

Chinuch (Dedication)

Blessing new home by affixing mezuzot and reciting Psalm xxx. The word also means "preparation," Hebrew education.

Chirek

Vowel dot under Hebrew letters.

Chiyyah (Hiyya) bar Abba

Tanna of second century who helped complete text to Tosefta.

Chmielnicki

(1595-1675)

Revolutionary Cossack hetman, perpetrator of bloody pogroms in seventeenth century Poland, Lithuania, and Ukraine.

Chokhmah

Wisdom.

Chokhmat ha-Ibbur

Science of intercallation.

Chol ha-Moed

Half-holidays—middle days of Passover and Sukkoth.

Cholent

(derived from French *chaleur*)

Dish of meat, beans, potatoes, and other vegetables, prepared on Friday and left simmering in oven for Sabbath consumption.

Chosen People

Much misunderstood appellation of the Jewish people; it implies no ascendancy over other men, but a chosenness to do good and love God.

Choshen

Silver breastplate suspended from tops of Torah roll. Often has holder containing name plate of the festivals, displayed on appropriate days.

Chovah

Religious duty.

Chronicles

Two final books of the Bible, recapitulating Hebrew history, the history of Judah, and the injunction against idolatry as treason to God.

Chuetas (bacon-eaters)

Derogatory term for descendants of Marranos, still practicing Jewish rituals. Remnant in Majorca.

Chukkot ha-Goyim

"Customs of the nations (gentiles)" to be avoided by Jews, lest they diminish Jewish loyalties. This would include observance of Christmas or other Christian festivals.

Chumash

(A fifth)

The Books of Moses; Pentateuch.

Chuppah

Canopy under which pair stand at wedding ceremony, symbol of home to be established.

Chutzpah

Nerve; impudence.

Circumcision

Circumcision, or amputation of the male prepuce, is one of the oldest as well as most widespread of customs. It is or was practiced (although with many variations as to method, age at the time of circumcision, who may perform the rite, etc.) among Jews, Mohammedans, Egyptians, Polynesians, the Indian tribes of the New World, and many of the primitive tribes of Africa and Australia. It is estimated that one-seventh of the male population of the world is circumcised. Many theories are advanced to explain the origin and purpose of this custom; such as (a) for hygienic reasons, (b) as a mark of tribal affiliation, (c) as a preparation for sexual life, (d) as a means of sanctifying the generative faculties, (e) as a sacrifice redeeming the male from the god who gave him life. For the Jews circumcision is one of the most important of the 613 commandments. It was interpreted as a sign of the covenant between God and Israel and, therefore, indispensable as a mark of affiliation with the latter (cf. Gen. 17:10-14; Ex. 12:40-49). In the Talmud, many prescriptions are laid down regulating the act of circumcision. It may be performed even on the Sabbath, if that is the eighth day after birth. It consists of (a) milah, the amputation of the prepuce, (b) periah, the baring of the glans, (c) metzitzah, staunching the flow of blood. Appropriate benedictions are recited before and after the circumcision and the child is given a name at this time. The circumcision ceremony is usually followed by a festive meal, at which a special grace is recited in which reference is made to this event.

Clothing

In Biblical times Jews' clothing was identical with that of non-Jews except for interdiction of mixed wool and linen (shaatnez). Observant Jews still wear fringes (tzitzit) on corners of special undergarment—Numbers 15:38. Prescribed clothing for Jews first ordered by Mohammedans, eighth century. First similar order in Western world by Pope Innocent III (1215)—pointed "Jew hat." Yellow spot or ring on coat mandatory in Germany to eighteenth century. Eastern European Jews developed customs of broad-brimmed fur hat and long black kaftan (coat), with silks for holidays.

Cohen

Most used Jewish name, from Hebrew word for "priest."

Cohen, Hermann

(1842-1918)

The basis of Cohen's philosophy was that God made truth

possible. His system of critical idealism dealt with the logic of pure knowledge, the ethics of pure will, and the aesthetics of pure feeling. He emphasized that basically his ethical philosophy was connected with the teachings of Judaism. For many years he was a professor at the University of Marburg. Upon his retirement at the age of seventy, he spent his last years as a teacher of Jewish philosophy at the Institute for the Science of Judaism in Berlin. In addition to educating rabbinical students, he directed discussions each Friday for the benefit of the general public. Many non-Jewish scholars attended these, eager to profit by Cohen's answers to questions concerning the whole range of science and philosophy. His method for teaching the rudiments of philosophy to beginners was greatly admired. He listened patiently to his students, helped them articulate their thoughts and express themselves methodically. He regarded his technique of discussion with beginners as test of his doctrine wherein thought was "pure creation," not the result but the condition of experience. His interpretations of the critiques of Kant, in his early years, gave new direction to the Neo-Kantian movement. The idea of God occupies the central position in his philosophy of critical idealism. The idea contains the connotation of a basic harmony between the structure of the universe and the aspirations of mankind. Cohen's introduction of the idea of God into his philosophy is an attempt to satisfy the longing of men to believe that the ethical ideal is real in a more solid sense than that of an aesthetic ideal. God as an idea is neither alive nor a person. He can be discovered by the processes of reason itself. Religion, properly so-called, arises with the emergence of the ethical consciousness. The "function" of God is not to provide prosperity, or even happiness, but to aid the efforts of men to discriminate between right and wrong. The idea of God assures the continued existence of nature for the ethical work of man. Religion is wholly the result of the fiat of man. It is a stratagem of the spirit, a psychological instrument employed by man for the sake of improving his character. Man does the work of redemption. God is the sign or the name, signifying attainment of a victory over sin. Religion alone is capable of producing the ideal of individuality. The conception of sin is in principle applicable to an individual only, not to a social group. The cultivation of intellectual faculties is a religious duty. The religious philosophy of Cohen had idealistic, positivistic, and humanistic elements derived from his intuition concerning the objective validity of ethical experience. (W) THE RELIGION OF REASON FROM THE SOURCES OF JUDAISM; RELIGION IN THE SYSTEM OF PHILOSOPHY.

Cohen, Morris Raphael

(1880-1947)

When Cohen was a boy in Minsk, Russia, he was called Kallyeleh, the Yiddish equivalent of moron. At the age of twelve, he emigrated to the United States. People from Cohen's native town were considerably astonished to hear, in later years, that the so-called moron was generally acknowledged as one of the strongest intellectual forces in American education and philosophy. Many of the greatest contemporary minds – Einstein, Woodbridge, Dewey, Russell, Oliver Wendell Holmes, Jr., and Cardozo—considered Cohen their equal. His disciples admired his wisdom and his teaching methods. His cardinal virtue was his integrity of mind and conscience. He was outstanding as a logician and mathematician, and was chiefly responsible for the renaissance of philosophy in American law. Cohen's interest in the philosophy of law and religion dated back to his "moronic" boyhood, when he was educated in Biblical and Talmudic law and read Maimonides and Judah Halevi's KUZARI. As a young man, he was attracted to Marxian socialism, but his strong belief in democracy helped him to discover other ways of serving the common good and acting in accordance with his social conscience. Felix Adler influenced his approach to ethics; but Cohen was essentially a logician, devoted to mathematical logic and to the investigation of the relationship between science and philosophy. He characterized himself as a realistic rationalist who conceived of reason as "the use of both deductive and inductive inferences working upon the material of experience." He regarded reality as a category that belonged to science not religion.

Cohn, Tobias

(Metz, 1652–Jerusalem, 1729)

Physician to five sultans, he wrote on all sciences and on theology. Author of MAASEH TOBIYAH.

Confirmation

Generic term for Bar Mitzvah, but now applied to special graduation exercises of synagogue schools. Introduced by liberal and now adopted by conservative and some Orthodox synagogues.

Communist Party of Israel

Leftist political organization in Israel, following the Marxist-Leninist party line. Basically Arabic with only a sprinkling of paid agents of Jewish faith.

Conservative Judaism

Like Reform, Conservatism arose in Germany. Among formulators of its theology were Isaac Bernays (1792-1849) and Zacharias Frankel (1801-1875). American leadership centers in the Jewish Theological Seminary, New York. Though the movement has set forth no system of principles or dogmas, there is an understanding as to basic ideas and objectives. Conservative Judaism accepts the revealed authority of the Bible, of the Talmud (rabbinic), and of later commentators. However, it permits changes in observance, provided they are dictated by inner logic and do justice to the law. It tends to conserve traditional religious forms. Though prayer may be read in other tongues, Hebrew still dominates. Jewish history is studied seriously and critically. Observes dietary laws with slight relaxations. Observes festivals and Sabbaths much like the Orthodox. But it has adopted some customs of Reform, such as late Friday services, mixed pews, and collateral use of the vernacular in worship.

Conversion

Judaism accepts proselytes, but frowns upon missionarizing activity. A court of three rabbis must accept the convert. Liberal Jews instruct the candidate, but do not insist on the ritual bath or other requisites of traditional law.

Converso

Convert; Sephardic.

Cordovero, Moses

(Cordova, 1522–Safed, 1570)

Cabbalist, philosopher; systematized Zohar in PARDES RIMMONIM (*Garden of Pomegranates*).

Covenant

(OT "berith"; NT "diatheke")

One of the fundamental words in Biblical religion; a formula, originating as the legal basis of society, used to describe the special relationship between God and people. A.) OT conception: A discussion may be divided into two parts: the covenant as (1) the basis of community, and as (2) theological terminology. 1. In early Israelite society as in all nomadic or semi-nomadic society covenants between men and between groups were the legal arrangements which made peaceful community relations possible. In the OT the expression most frequently used is: X cut a covenant with Y. Other verbs are occasionally employed, but "cut" is the most common, and probably refers to sacrificial rites which originally initiated the agreement. Two familiar illustrations of O.T. covenants are those made between David and Jonathan (I Sam. 18:3, 20:8, and 23:18) and between Jacob and Laban (Gen. 31:44-45). In the latter the rite consisted of setting up a pillar (E source), or heap of stones (J source), vows, sacrificial offering, and community meal. It is important to notice that the deity (or deities?—cf. vs. 53) of the respective groups was made a party to the agreement and would see that it was kept (n.b. the Mizpah Benediction). Thus the covenant was absolutely binding and could never be safely broken. Righteousness in the OT, therefore, was primarily maintenance of the covenant, while sin was its transgression, breach of an agreement. 2. With this background the theological significance of the word is clear. The sources agree that in the period of the Wandering, Conquest, and Settlement, what held the various groups of the people of Israel together was a religious bond or covenant (cf. Exod. 24 and Josh. 24), made of their own free will with Yahweh. God chose Israel to be His people, and Israel chose Him to be her God. Israel was thus conscious of a special contractual relationship existing between her and God, a relationship carrying with it certain obligations, the keeping of which meant life or death, blessing or curse (Dt. 30:5ff.). Later writers, especially Hosea, Jeremiah, Ezekiel, and the authors of Deuteronomy and Priestly Writings, made frequent use of this conception. Israel, it was claimed, had broken the covenant (Hos. 6:7, 8:1; Jer. 11:1ff., 34:18). An explanation was accordingly provided for the problem of suffering, though to some it was not entirely adequate, since it raised the problem of theodicy (cf. Hab. and Job). A fundamental difference of opinion between religious leaders in the OT was in regard to the precise obligations which the covenant with God entailed. While the priestly group emphasized the external prescriptions of the law, in particular the ritualistic law, the greatest of the prophets were more concerned with deeper ethical and religious issues, a point of view which found one of its highest expressions in the prediction of a new covenant, not like that made on Sinai which had been broken by Israel, but one which was to be written on the hearts of men (Jer. 31:31ff.). B.) NT conception: The Greek word "*diatheke*" was most commonly employed in Hellenistic Greek for "will," "testament," but in the LXX and NT it is also used to designate the OT idea of covenant. The most frequent use of the latter in the NT is in the Pauline writings and in the Epistle to the Hebrews, where the contrast is made between the Old Covenant of law and the New Covenant in Christ. The OT conception, expressing comprehension of the divine election and the binding relationship of the elect to God, is not developed in the NT. The idea of covenant there is used rather to clarify the difference between Christianity and Judaism (cf. Luke 22:20; I Cor. 11:25; Gal. 3:15ff.; Heb. 8ff.).

Covenant of Abraham

Rite of circumcision enjoined on Abraham and his descendants.

Covering head

Traditional custom demands covered head at all times, particularly at prayers and meals. Reform practice permits uncovered head in all circumstances.

Crescas, Hasdai

(1340-1410)

Like almost all Jewish philosophers of the Middle Ages, Crescas developed his philosophy in the face of persecution and imminent personal danger. He was born in Barcelona and was denounced and victimized there, imprisoned and fined, despite the recognition of his innocence. He moved and settled in Saragossa, where he declined appointment as rabbi of the congregation. He then became an authority on Jewish law and ritual tradition, and often intervened diplomatically on behalf of his co-religionists in Aragon and neighboring kingdoms. In a letter from him to the Jews of Avignon, he described the personal pain he and other Jews endured during the persecution of Jews in Spain. It was during this Inquisition period (1391), that he lost his only son. Crescas did not content himself with bemoaning the fate of the Jews.

He endeavored to defend the spirit and doctrines of Judaism against its religious and philosophical opponents. His criticism of Christianity, written in Spanish, is lost, except for those fragments which were translated into Hebrew by Joseph ibn Shemtob in 1451. Crescas' principal work, OR ADONAI (*The Light of God*), completed in 1410, the year of his death, was of great consequence. It refuted Neo-Platonism and Aristotle, and implied a sharp criticism of Gersonides and Maimonides because of their efforts to reconcile Judaism with Greek philosophy. Crescas rejected Aristotle's physics, metaphysics, and axiology. He defended the cause of Judaism with a spiritual originality, radicalism, and courage uncommon in the history of the Middle Ages. The importance of his thinking was by no means confined to the history of Jewish philosophy. His rejection of Aristotle, by stating that "there are no other worlds" than the one system in which the earth is situated, inspired such Christian thinkers as Nicholas Cusanus, Giordano Bruno, Marsilio Ficino, and Pico della Mirandola. There is little doubt that Spinoza was indebted to Crescas for his concept of the universe.

Crusades

A series of holy wars to recapture Palestine from the Moslems, beginning in 1095 and ending after 1200. While the motives of some of the Christians were undoubtedly noble, adventure- and loot-seeking Crusaders quickly turned some of the Crusades into murderous pillage of European Jewry.

Customs

See MINHAG.

Cyrus

Conqueror of Medes, Lydia, and Babylonia, this ruler of Persia permitted Jews to return to Palestine from Babylon, 538 B.C.E.

D

D

Symbol used for the author (s) of the Book of Deuteronomy and for a school of historians or editors of the century following publication of Deuteronomy (621 B.C.E.) who employed the same vocabulary and style as that book, and were imbued with similar religious viewpoints. These editors were responsible for editions of Joshua, Judges, I and II Kings, Jeremiah, and possibly other books.

Dachau

German extermination camp near Munich. See AUSCHWITZ.

Dagesh

Center dot which changes or doubles pronunciation of Hebrew letter.

Daggatum

Moroccan nomads of Jewish ancestry and faith, living among the Tuareg, but not assimilating with them.

Dan

One of twelve sons of Jacob; a tribe.

Daniel

Hebrew book with large Aramaic enclave 2:4a-7:28. The latter is presumably somewhat older "Eastern" material, hurriedly adapted to new use in Palestine by revisions in chapters 2 and

7 and Hebrew introduction 1:1-2:4a and additional visions, ch. 8f, in the crisis under Antiochus Epiphanes (175-163 B.C.). The book, as a whole, is composed of two parts: 1-6, the story; 7-12, the visions of Daniel. Historical errors (Belshazzar not last king of Babylon; Darius not first ruler after fall of Babylon) make sixth-century origin of stories impossible. Dating of present book can be determined from visions, especially "prophetic" survey of history of Greek kingdoms in chapter 11, which becomes genuinely predictive in 11:40f. Of particular importance because of its influence on Jesus and the primitive church is the vision of chapter 7, with its figure of the "one like a Son of Man." The book's acceptance of the doctrine of the resurrection of the dead (12:2-3) and the later Jewish angelology is also noteworthy.

Darius

King of Persia (522-486), who assisted Zerubbabel in rebuilding the Temple.

Darshan

Rabbinic preacher ("interpreter").

Dathan

Conspired with his brother Abiram against Moses and Aaron.

Davar

Organ of Histadruth (General Federation of Jewish Labor [Mapai]) in Israel.

David

Second king of Judah and Israel; warrior, poet, harpist; about 1000 B.C.E. *Presumed* founder of messianic line. Like Moses, David was a shepherd before becoming a leader of his people. As conqueror of Jerusalem and unifier of his nation, he was the most colorful of Biblical heroes and authors. His career covered the killing of wild animals as a boy, the heroic killing of the Philistine giant Goliath, his musical service at the court of King Saul, the later antipathy of Saul which made him a mercenary and captain of outlaws, a magnanimity which more than once spared the pursuing king's life, and a life wherein great sin and saintly devotion to the Lord were extraordinarily mingled. David remains the most human and beloved of the kings.

David ben Samuel ha-Levi

(1586-1667)

Lemberg rabbi who wrote TURE ZAHAV ("*Taz*") on the Shulchan Arukh.

Day of Atonement

See ATONEMENT, DAY OF.

Day of Yahweh

(1) Day popularly anticipated (between time of Solomon and Amos) when Yahweh would bring unprecedented prosperity, intervene to eliminate foreign enemies, and re-establish His nation on a glorious scale even surpassing Solomon's time. (2) Amos and his successors reversed this. Yahweh would come, but to punish His sinful nation by immediate military conquest. (3) In postexilic time the Day of Yahweh concept was eschatologized and referred to as the Judgment Day. An editor from this school inserted excerpts here and there throughout the prophetic writings, giving their already fulfilled predictions new validity for the "Great Day."

Dayan

Rabbinical judge.

Dead Sea

In legend, created by flooding of Sodom and Gomorrah. To the Arabs, Sea of Lot.

Dead Sea Scrolls

Archeological discovery of recent years in caves overlooking Dead Sea—parts of Bible and other documents.

Deborah

Judge of Israel, whose General Sisera defeated Barak and liberated her people. The Song of Deborah is one of the great Biblical documents.

Decalogue

(Gr. *deka,* "ten"; *logos,* "word, matter")

The Ten Commandments held to be the foundation of Christian morality, and said to have been given to Moses by God at Mount Sinai, written on table(t)s of stone: Exod. 31:18; 34:1. Found in their most familiar form in Exod. 20:2-17 and (with a different reason given for the fourth) in Deut. 5:6-21. A different version specifically designated (Exod. 34:28) as "the ten words" (Eng., "commandments"), but dealing only with festivals and offerings, appears in Exod. 34:10-26; it is said to be what was written on the second pair of stone tablets after Moses had broken the first, which contained the "ten words" of Exod. 20:2ff. No explanation is given of the inconsistency, which is doubtless due to the unresolved claim of priority of each version. Still other by-forms of the Decalogue appear in Deut. 27 and in Levit. 19. The several forms of the Decalogue apparently were "threshold liturgies," whereby worshipers at different sanctuaries and in different periods acknowledged the essential requirements of Yahweh worship (cf. Psalms 15; 24:3-6; 118:20; and the place of the Ten Commandments in the Anglican office of Holy Communion). The reason for the "ten" is mnemonic. The variety witnesses to this usage as characteristic from the earliest times, but makes the ascription of any single form to Moses precarious. The Decalogue of Exod. 20–Deut. 5 was evidently in familiar use both in Israel and in Judah in the time of the classical Prophets (Jer. 7:9; Hos. 4:2), and is commonly held to embody their teaching. Since, however, the Prophets represented a renewal of the prophetism of Moses there is no sufficient reason to deny the possibility that this Decalogue, in the terse original form preserved by the 6th, 7th and 8th commandments or "words" may be Mosaic in origin. See TORAH.

Decapolis

The ten Hellenic cities in Palestine.

Deitch

German: what an East European Jew would call one aping Western manners.

Delilah

Samson's treacherous wife.

Delmedigo, Elijah

(1460-1497)

Italian Jewish philosopher who opposed Chasidism; wrote BECHINAT HA-DAT (*Examination of Religion*).

Derekh Eretz ("Way of the Earth")

Principles of ethics or etiquette.

Derush

Interpretation of Biblical or Talmudic text.

Deuteronomy

Fifth (last) Book of Moses. Recapitulation of Moses' story; exhortations to duty; farewell address of Moses, and appointment of Joshua as successor.

Devarim

Deuteronomy.

Diaspora ("Dispersion")

Referring to Jews in voluntary or forced "exile" from the Holy Land, particularly in the era of Jewish expulsion from their homeland after the destruction of Jerusalem at the hands of Titus (70 C.E.).

Dibbuk (Adherent)

Spirit of deceased that enters body of living person; cabbalistic idea. Famous drama by Anski.

Dietary Laws

Frequently and erroneously taken as the mainstay of Jewish observance. Dietary laws are mainly of hygienic and ethical origin (against pork eating, blood drinking, etc.). Liberal Jews as a rule disregard these laws of *kashrut*. The essence of Judaism lies in observance of the holy spirit underlying its high-minded laws and precepts.

Din

Judgment; religious law or prescription.

Disraeli, Benjamin

(1804-1881)

British prime minister; Earl of Beaconsfield. Builder of British Empire under Queen Victoria. Novelist of distinction. Though a convert, friend of Israel and of early Zionist striving.

Divorce

Traditionally, a religious divorce (*gett*) must be obtained to dissolve a religious marriage. Liberal Jews accept civil divorce alone.

Djadid ul-Islam

"New Moslems": Small sect of Crypto-Jews (Marranos) who were forced in 1838 in the town of Meshed, Persia, to adopt the Moslem faith. Secretly, however, they continued to observe Jewish ritual.

Domus Conversorum

Hostel for converts established in London 1232 by Henry III, and discontinued in 1891.

Donmeh

Renegades; Judeo-Moslem sect descended from followers of Shabbetai Zevi.

Dov Ber of Meseritz

See BAER.

Dreidel

See TRENDEL.

Dreyfus, Alfred

(1859-1935)

French Jewish officer falsely accused of treason. Later exonerated through efforts of Zola, Clemenceau, and other liberals. His case strongly affected Theodor Herzl.

Dropsie, Moses Aaron

(1821-1905)

Philadelphia philanthropist whose will provided for establishment in that city of the Dropsie College for Hebrew and Cognate Learning.

Dual allegiance

A bugaboo of anti-Semites and self-hating Jews. American Jews are completely loyal to the land of the free and the democratic way of life. They would be poor Americans if they showed no compassion for their coreligionists, and also relatives, living in Israel. American civilization upholds close family life; to question the devotion of American Jewry toward their Israeli brethren is similar to the question as to how one can love both father and mother.

Dubnow, Simon

(1860-1944)

Russian sociologist and historian, murdered by Nazis. Author of much translated HISTORY OF THE JEWISH PEOPLE.

Duchan

The platform from which priests blessed the people in the Temple. The blessing was said ceremonially with face covered and arms uplifted. The word is now used to indicate the blessing service itself.

Dunam

Land measure, about one-fourth acre, in Israel.

Dura Europos

City on Euphrates with ruins dated to 265 C.E. Seat of synagogue containing unique fresco cycle.

Duran, Profiat

(end 14th century)

Grammarian; philosopher; forced convert who returned to Judaism; wrote historical letter to renegades, AL TEHI KAAVOTECHA (*Be Not Like Your Forefathers*).

Dymov, Ossip (Perelman)

(1878—)

Yiddish writer born in Bialystok; since 1913 in U.S. (W) *Shema Yisroel, Revolutions of the Sun.*

E

E

Symbol used for one of the component narratives of certain OT books, derived from the initial letter of the divine name Elohim which it employs before the revelation of Yahweh to Moses. It is found in Genesis–Judges, and possibly also in I, II Samuel. E was written in the northern kingdom, Ephraim, probably in the eighth century B.C.E. The existence of E as a separate narrative has recently been contested by some scholars (Volz, Rudolph), who assign certain parts of the supposed E Document to other documents (J, D, P) and consider other parts as editorial matter.

Eber

Great-grandson of Shem, from whose name "Hebrew" is derived.

Ecclesiastes (Kohelet)

Biblical work—"The Preacher" —ascribed to Solomon; philosophical pessimism; canonicity disputed to late period.

Edels, Samuel Eliezer

(Posen, 1555–Volhynia, 1631)

Known as Maharsha, this scholar sought to solve Talmudic difficulties in his CHIDDUSHE HALAKHOT VA'AGGADOT.

Edom

Genesis tells us that the country which was inhabited by Esau and his descendants was called "the field of Edom."

Einhorn, David

(Bavaria, 1809–New York, 1879)

German rabbi, preacher, and theological writer; leader of the Reform movement in America.

Einstein, Albert

(1879-1955)

The overwhelming majority of scientists continually testify that Einstein has accomplished "one of the greatest generalizations of all time" and "has revolutionized our nineteenth century concepts not only of astronomy, but also of the nature of time, space, and of the fundamental ideas of science." Modern humanity reveres Einstein as one of its profoundest thinkers, as well as a man of the highest intellectual integrity, free of personal ambition, an intrepid fighter for human rights, social justice, and social responsibility. In the few decades that had passed between the time that Einstein had made his theory of relativity known to the public and his seventieth birthday, more than five thousand books and pamphlets in every language have been published about him and his ideas, his fame spread internationally after he predicted that the deflection of light in a gravitational field would occur in 1916 and 1919. He had and still has opponents, some of whom were prejudiced against him because he remained conscious of his Jewish origin. But humble people throughout the world are comforted by the knowledge that Einstein, whose thoughts pervade the universe, felt with all who suffer from oppression and persecution. Seldom has it happened that any man has become so popular, even though his theory is largely beyond popular imagination and common-sense thought. While the achievements of Copernicus, Galileo, Newton, and Darwin have been, at least in broad outline, explicable to the public, it has been impossible up to the present time to translate Einstein's theory of relativity adequately into the non-technical language of popular literature. The most important consequence of Einstein's special theory of relativity for scientific and philosophical thought has been the change in the concepts of time and space. Einstein destroyed the assumption that there is a single all-embracing time in which all events in the universe have their place. He has shown that "it is impossible to determine absolute motion by any experiment whatever." As long as time and space are measured separately, there always remains a kind of subjectivity which affects not only human observers but all other things. Time and space, which for classical physics are absolute constituents of the world, are conceived by Einsteinian physics as dependent upon each other, forming a relationship which can be analyzed in many different ways into what is referred to as spatial distance or lapse of time. Time which previously had been regarded as a cosmic measure is presented by Einstein as "local time" connected with the motion of the earth. He conceives of time as so completely analogous to the three dimensions of space that physics can be transformed into a kind of four-dimensional geometry. On the other hand, the special theory of relativity confers an absolute meaning on a magnitude, namely the velocity of light, which had only a relative significance in classical physics. After this special theory, Einstein formulated his general theory of relativity which offers new explanations of the size of the universe, of gravitation and inertia. Einstein's achievements are by no means limited to the special and general theories of relativity. He was awarded the Nobel Prize in 1922 for his studies in photo-chemical equivalents. Later, he took a leading part in the investigation of atomic energy. On many occasions, he had expressed his personal views on problems of daily life, contemporary history, war, peace, education, religion, science and the fate of the Jews. Many of these views are collected in his books, THE WORLD AS I SEE IT, OUT OF MY LATER YEARS and ESSAYS IN SCIENCE.

El

"The Mightiest"; name of God.

El Male Rachamim

"Lord, full of compassion"—memorial prayer chanted for the dead. Recited at Jahrzeit or Yizkor.

Eldad ha-Dani

Ninth-century traveler, who wrote fanciful tales of the lost Ten Tribes living in Ethiopia, and encircled by a fabled river, the Sambatyon.

Elephantine

Island in southern Nile, from which valuable papyri of the Persian period were recovered.

Eliezer ben Hyrcanus

Disciple of Jochanan ben Zaccai; one of the greatest tannaim, who created and headed academy at Lydda. Flourished 100 C.E. Also a member of the great Sanhedrin under Gamaliel the Second in Javneh.

Elijah

Prophet of Yahweh, living in the ninth century B.C.E. (I Kings 17-19; II Kings 1-2). A religious and political influence, he precipitated the fall of the house of Ahab and indirectly prepared the prophetic movement of Amos and Hosea.

Elijah ben Solomon

(1720-1797)

The famed Gaon of Wilna, master of all Jewish knowledge and of mathematics and the sciences; a rational thinker, he vigorously opposed Chasidism.

Elijah's seat

Chair of honor for Sandek of baby to be circumcised.

Elisha

Disciple and successor of Elijah.

Elisha ben Abuya

(2nd century)

Talmudic scholar called Acher ("The Other") because of his deviations from religious norms.

Elohim

Name of God, plural of Eloha —"The Powerful."

Elohist

Designation of presumed author of those portions of the Pentateuch using Elohim as name of God.

Elul

Twelfth month of Jewish year.

Emancipation

Of Western Jew began in U.S. 1776; in Europe at French National Convention, 1791. The American liberation was immediate and permanent; in Europe there were slowness and relapse. Under modern Hitler, 1933-1945, and under Stalin and his successors, Jewish religious freedom has been curtailed or obliterated.

Emek Habakhah

The Valley of Weeping.

Emet

Truth.

End of Days (Acharit ha-Yamim)

Day of judgment; battle of Gog and Magog; coming of Messiah; resurrection; eternal peace in New Jerusalem (Isaiah 40-66; Ezekiel 36-48).

Enoch

The seventh of the ten antediluvian patriarchs of Gen. 5. The Biblical record tells that he lived three hundred and sixty-five years; "and Enoch walked with God; and he was not, for God had taken him." This Biblical record furnished the motif for two Jewish, post-Biblical, noncanonical, apocalyptic books. Both recount the journeyings of Enoch, under divine guidance, through the entire earth and through the seven heavens, and the divine revelation to him of all the mysteries of heaven and earth, that he, in turn, might reveal them to mankind. The older and larger book, usually designated I Enoch, was of composite authorship, written in Palestine, probably in Aramaic, between the third and first centuries B.C.E., and is preserved complete only in an Ethiopic translation, though some fragments of the ancient Greek translation likewise exist. II Enoch was probably written in Egypt, in Greek, during the first half-century C.E. It has survived only in a Slavonic translation.

Ephod

Luxurious vestment of the high priest.

Eretz (Land)

When used alone, this word refers to Palestine or Israel (Eretz Yisrael).

Eretz Yisrael

Land of Israel; Biblical designation of Canaan.

Erev

Eve.

Erusin

Betrothal.

Eruv (Mixture; Union)

Means of alleviating difficulties attendant upon strict religious observance on Sabbaths and festivals; legal fictions whereby partitions or wires render public places (wherein naught may be carried on the Sabbath) into private territory; food may be placed at the end of 2,000 paces from the city (the permitted Sabbath journey), so that under necessity a man may walk still further; a whole community is made part of the house by placing a loaf of bread to which all contributed in the yard; and similar provisions.

Eshet Chayil

Woman of valor or merit.

Essenes (Healers)

Ascetic communistic sect that disappeared at destruction of the Temple. May have influenced the life and ideas of the Christian Jesus.

Esther (Hadassah)

Queen of King Ahasuerus who, with her cousin and guardian Mordecai saved Persian Jewry from annihilation by Haman. Book of Bible; heroine of Purim.

Esther, Scroll of

Bible book in decorative scrolls for public reading on Purim, the festival created in the Bible story.

Ethical Culture Societies

The Ethical Culture movement was inaugurated by Professor Felix Adler (1851-1933) in New York City, on May 15, 1876. Adler had come to this country as a child of four from the Rhineland, and after taking his degree at Columbia College became instructor in oriental languages and literature at Cornell University. He had been trained to succeed his father as rabbi of Temple Emanuel in New York, but revolting against the theology and ceremonialism of the Hebrew religion, he founded, with the support of a few sympathizers who left the synagogue with him, a society pledged "to assert the supreme importance of the ethical factor in all relations of life, personal, social, national, and international, apart from any theological or metaphysical considerations."

Ethnarch

Greek title; head of Jewish community in Alexandria; successors of Herod were so named.

Etrog

Citron, one of Palestinian plants used to celebrate Sukkoth; must be perfect in surface and stem. Often kept in highly ornate containers.

Etz Chaim

Wooden roller on which Torah is wound; there are two for each scroll.

Euthanasia

Disapproved by spirit of Jewish law.

Eve

From word for life (Chavah); first woman.

Excommunication (Cherem)

Anathema placed upon persons and materials, once powerful, then abused, and now rarely invoked. See CHEREM.

Exegesis

"Exegesis" is the transliteration of the Greek *exegesis,* which would mean "narrative," "translation," or "interpretation." It is in the last sense that the noun is used in theology; exegesis is interpretation, more particularly and usually interpretation of Scripture. In technical parlance the word describes the actual interpretation of a concrete passage, while the general principles of Biblical interpretation are classed together as hermeneutics. In the OT period the official interpreters of the Law were the priests (Hag. 2:10-13), who in the "intermediate" and NT periods were succeeded by the scribes; especially the scribes belonging to the Pharisaic party, who alone continued after C.E. 70. Their hermeneutic principles maintained that the Law, being divine, foresaw all possible problems and so by fresh interpretation could be indefinitely expanded; the theory that produced the overwhelming luxuriance of Talmudic Judaism. And this method was aided by allegory, Greek in origin but adopted by the Jews before the Christian era, which sought a spiritual sense underlying Scripture; Philo of Alexandria exhibits the lengths to which allegory could be carried. The first Christian exegesis followed the contemporary precedents unquestioningly (1 Cor. 9:9-10; Gal. 4:21-31, etc.), and allegory in the second century reached fantastic heights, controlled only by insistence that "orthodox" theology must not be violated.

Exilarch (Resh Galuta)

Head of exilic Babylonian Jewry. Also called Prince of Captivity.

Exile

See DIASPORA.

Exile Festival

The day added to each Biblically ordained festival day (Passover, Shavuoth, Sukkoth) for the lands of exile.

Exodus

The second book of the OT, containing the account of the oppression of the Israelites in Egypt and their exodus from that land and journey to Mt. Sinai under the leadership of Moses (chapters 1-18); and the account of various events at Mt. Sinai, including the making of the covenant and the promulgation of certain laws (chapters 19-40). Although Moses is traditionally considered the author, it is a composite work by J, E, and P. Chapters 25-31, 35-40 are exclusively P material; the rest of the book is a combination of the three sources. Exodus is of special interest, for it records the revelation of Yahweh to Moses (ch. 3 JE; 6:2-13 P), and the giving of the Ten Commandments. The ethical Decalogue is found in chapter 20, usually attributed to E, but a "ritual decalogue" was discovered by Goethe in chapter 34, and many scholars have maintained that this was the original Mosaic Decalogue. This is improbable, since the prescriptions of this chapter are applicable almost exclusively to a settled agrarian society; if Moses did not give the familiar Ten Commandments of chapter 20 (in a shorter form, with restricted application), we do not know what laws he promulgated. The date of the exodus has been the subject of extensive debate. No theory has been advanced which fits all the archaeological and Biblical data, but a date in the thirteenth century B.C.E. seems most satisfactory in view of the archaeological evidence.

Exodus from Egypt

Commemorated in prayer services; Song of Miriam is included in morning prayers.

Expulsions of Jews

A common fate of the people. From England, 1290; France, 1306; Spain, 1492.

Eyebeschutz, Jonathan

(Cracow, 1690–Altona, 1764)

Talmudist, cabbalist, head of Prague Yeshivah, rabbi of Altona, Hamburg, and Wandsbeck, writer of legal and homiletic works, called a Shabbetarian by Rabbi Jacob Emden in a famous controversy. Author of *Urim Vetumin, Kereti U-feleti.*

Ezekiel

Book of a priest who was among those deported with Jehoiachim (II Kings 24:15) 598 B.C.E. and was called to be a prophet in the fifth year after that event (1:2). The last date of his prophecy is the twenty-seventh year (29:17), 571 B.C.E. The book consists of three parts: 1-24—prophecies against Israel (Judah) and Jerusalem; 25-32—prophecies against foreign nations (secondarily placed in the present position, prophecies 24:26-27 are continued in 33:21-22); 34-48—salutary prophecies for the Israel of the future (40-48, the vision of the new temple, city, and Holy Land forming a distinct unit within the section). The book has been a storm center of criticism in late years. Radical solutions such as Torrey's (a third century B.C.E. pseudepigraph!) have added to the confusion. The "authentic" pieces giving experiences or utterances of the prophet are all dated except 12:1-10, where the date may have been lost (through transposition?), and are arranged in chronological order (now slightly disturbed; cf. 29:19, a later date than 40:1). But each date applies only to the first unit following it; other distinct pieces subjoined to dated units are suspected of having been placed there redactionally, and their authenticity must be judged separately. That the book has been much expanded by other hands, notably also in chapters 40-48, is certain. But even a critically "reduced" book will show that Ezekiel was a man of great originality of thought and character. His influence on subsequent religious and theological development was large. He has been called the John Calvin of the OT. See GOG AND MAGOG.

Ezra

According to the record in Scripture, Ezra was leader of a caravan which returned from Babylonia to the Holy Land in the reign of Artaxerxes, King of Persia (Ezra 7:1). (It is usually assumed that this Artaxerxes is the first king of that name, and that the date of Ezra's arrival in Palestine is thus fixed at 458 B.C.E. It has, however, been suggested that the Artaxerxes referred to is the second, and that the date of Ezra's arrival should be fixed at 297 B.C.E.) The authenticity of Ezra's memoirs, now included in the Book which bears his name, is being defended with increasing vigor by Bible students; and the tendency to declare his whole existence mythological is definitely weakening under the pressure of new studies in the Biblical text and more precise information regarding Persian life. Ezra's fame, so far as Judaism is concerned, rests only secondarily on the main incident recorded in his memoirs—his forcible separation of the Judaic from the heathen wives whom many of them had married. Tradition attributes to him the repromulgation of the Pentateuch as the accepted and binding discipline of Law for all Israel. In this sense, Ezra is held to have completed the work initiated by Moses, a millennium before him. It seems certain that Ezra was an important factor in the establishment of synagogue worship, the custom of reading the Law as part of this service, and the ultimate substitution of the student of the Law for the prophet as the moral guide of the people. In this sense, undoubtedly, Ezra was the founder of rabbinic legalism.

F

Falaquera, Shem-Tov ben Joseph

(1225-1290)

Follower of Maimonides, who lived either in Spain or France; writer of harmonizations of Judaism and Aristotelianism.

Falashas

A tribe of dark-skinned Jews living in Ethiopia for many centuries. Their origin is unknown, but they claim ancient descent. They call themselves "Beta-Israel" (House of Israel) but the natives call them Falashas, or "exiles," "immigrants." Although diverging from standard Jewish practice at many points, they hold steadfast by Mosaic Judaism, based on an Ethiopic version of the Pentateuch, but considerably modified by their complete ignorance of Hebrew. They are strict monotheists and lead a highly moral life. Living completely apart from the natives, they will not allow anyone outside their group into their hutlike homes or their synagogues (mesgid). They strictly observe laws of ritual purity and therefore establish themselves near running water. Their leaders are divided into "menokassie" (Nazarites), "kahens" (priests), and "dabteras" (learned men), who are all nonprofessionals.

Falk, Hayyim Samuel Jacob

(Bavaria, c. 1708–London, 1782)

Mystic cabbalist, known as the "Baal Shem of London." The Orthodox rabbi, Jacob Emden, denounced him as a follower of the false Messiah, Shabbetai Zevi.

Falk, Jacob Joshua ben Zevi Hirsch

(Poland, 1680—Germany, 1756)

A leading Talmudist of his day, author of *Pene Yehoshua* (*Countenance of Joshua*), commentaries on the Talmud.

Falk, Joshua ben Alexander Hakohen

(Lublin, c. 1550–Lemberg, 1614)

Talmudist and head of the Lemberg Yeshivah. His major work, *Sefer Meirath Enayim* (*Book of the Enlightenment of the Eyes*), is a commentary on the Shulchan Arukh.

Falkensohn, Issachar bar

(Poland, 1746–Ukraine, 1817)

Physician, poet and friend of Mendelssohn. His *Gedichte eines polnischen Juden* (*Poems of a Polish Jew*) reviewed by Goethe.

Familianten Law

Limitation of Jewish marriages in Bohemian crown lands, seventeenth and eighteenth centuries.

Fano, Immanuel

(1548-1620)

Italian rabbi and cabbalist.

Farband

Fraternal Poale Zion group.

Farchi, Estori ben Moses

(Spain, 1282–Palestine, 1357)

Traveler and archaeologist, first explorer of Palestine. His historical, archaeological, geographical and botanical findings collected in the *Kaftor va-Ferah* (*A Bud and a Flower*).

Farissol, Abraham ben Mordecai

(1451-1526)

French-Spanish scribe, geographer, translator, polemicist. He knew Columbus, and wrote Hebrew account of discovery of America. His MAGEN ABRAHAM defends Judaism against Islam and Christianity; most of his Biblical commentaries are still unpublished.

Fassel', Hirsch bar

(Moravia, 1802–Hungary, 1883)

One of the leaders of the Jewish Reform movement in Moravia, and author of numerous volumes on Mosaic and Talmudic law.

Fasting

In Hebrew, *tzom, taanit*—for penance or mourning. Pentateuch prescribes only Yom Kippur. A *taanit tzibbur* is a specially ordained community fast; major commemorative fastdays include Nissan 14, fast of the first-born; Tammuz 17, breach of Jerusalem's walls; Av 9, destruction of both Temples; Tishri 3, Fast of Gedaliah; Tevet 10, siege of Jerusalem; Adar 13, Fast of Esther.

Fat

The Torah contains detailed instructions concerning the fat of animals offered on the altar. The fat is to be burnt, under no circumstances may be eaten. This prohibition is closely linked with that forbidding the eating of blood, which is considered the seat of life.

Fattori

The three members of the executive body of the Jewish community in medieval Rome: Sindachi, Gonfalonieri, Fattori del Ghetto. They supervised internal community affairs and were responsible to the Vatican.

Felsenthal, Bernhard

(Germany, 1822–Chicago, 1908)

Leader and secretary of the Chicago Jewish Reform Society. His *Kol Kore Ba-Midbar: Uber Jüdische Reform* (*A Voice Calls in the Wilderness: On Jewish Reform*) was a plea for individual and congregational autonomy in religious affairs.

PLATE 17. Rabbi Moses ben Nachman
(Nachmanides–Ramban 1194-1270)

(Courtesy of Frank J. Darmstaedter)

PLATE 18. Isaac Abravanel (1437-1508)

(*A drawing by Arthur Szyk*)

PLATE 19. Joseph Caro (1488-1575)

Wahre und nach dem Leben getroffene Contrafe-ctur/ des jetzigen Jüdischen Groß-Propheten und gesalbten gekrönten König/ nach Gestalt alter Habit und Auffzug eigentlich entworffen/ &c. Der Prophet ist seines Alters 70. Jahr/ der König im Jahr seiner Jugend/ zwischen 15. und 25. so gesehen worden/ zu Cazzo den 26. Julij. Anno 1665. Und dann auch das aus dem Hebräischen verteutsche Jüdische Schreiben aus Jerusalem. Abgangen an die berühmte Judenschafft in Europa.

WIr Juden euere Brüder/ so nunmehro zu Jerusalem sind/ wünschen euch Juden unsern Brüdern/ so in Europa noch zerstreuet sind/ Glück und Heil; Und wie wir allezeit an euch in euer höchsten Zerstreuung in unser H. Stadt gedacht/ und solche euere und unsere allgemeine nothleydende Verachtung aufs eusserste nun eine geraume Zeit wehemühtig beklaget haben/ Als können wir wiederumb im Gegentheil/ euch lieben Brüder/ in gröster Hertzens-Freud nicht verhalten/ welcher massen/ nach dem wir lang gehoffet/ ein grosser Prophet aus Priesterlichem alten Jüdischen Stamm/ Namens Nathan Levi erwecket worden/ welcher nit nur allein unser altes Gesetz mit grosser Gewalt erörtert und beschirmet/ sondern auch/ voll seines Geistes/ die herrliche Geburt und Ankunfft unsers liebsten Messiæ/ welchen er dann neulich zum König gesalbet/ geoffenbahret/ und unserem Volck/ mit grossem Freuden-Geschrey vorblasen lassen/ zumalen wellen er uns hin und wider verstreute sammlen/ zusammen bringen/ wieder alle Gewalt unsere abgesagte Feind/ schützen und erretten wird/ wie dann allbereit Er unser neugebohrner Messias mit seinem Heiligen Propheten nicht nur grosse Wunder gethan/ sondern auch den bösen Raub-Vogel unsers gelobten Landes in höchste Bangigkeit gesetzet/ und auffs eheste gänzlich fällen und austreiben wird.

Demnach nun weil wir auff den fünff und zwantzigsten Tag des Monden Caslev / gedencken die Reinigung des lang verunseuberten Tempels zubegehen zu Jerusalem / als haben wir es euch/ aus ernstlichem Gebott unsers Königs/ anzeigen sollen/ auff daß ihr mit allen den eurigen wisset/ es gebühre euch dieses Fest mit zuhalten/ und sollen also/ nach dem ihr diesen Brieff gelesen/ und in euren ausländischen Synagogen/ vierzehen Tag und Nacht werdet gefastet und also euch geheiliget haben/ ins gesampt mit Weib und Kind euch zur Reis rüsten/ damit also ihr alle/ bey dem Gebott unsers Messiæ/ auffgesetzten Tag die Reinigung des Tempels mit begehen/ und darauff ferners das gelobte Land/ nach eurem grossen Wolgefallen/ bewohnen möget. Welchen nun ihr Jüdisches Heil angenehm / werden dieser Königlichen Citation nicht widerleben/ sondern in allem Gehorsam/ …eulich nachkommen/ darzu dann sich unser Messias/ Prophet und sämptliche Judenschafft in Jerusalem versehen.

Prophet Nathan.
sämptliche Judenschafft in Jerusalem.

Messias der Juden.

PLATE 20. Shabbetai Zevi (1626-1676) in His Messianic Getup.

(*Bust by Ewing*)

PLATE 21. Baruch Spinoza (1632-1677)

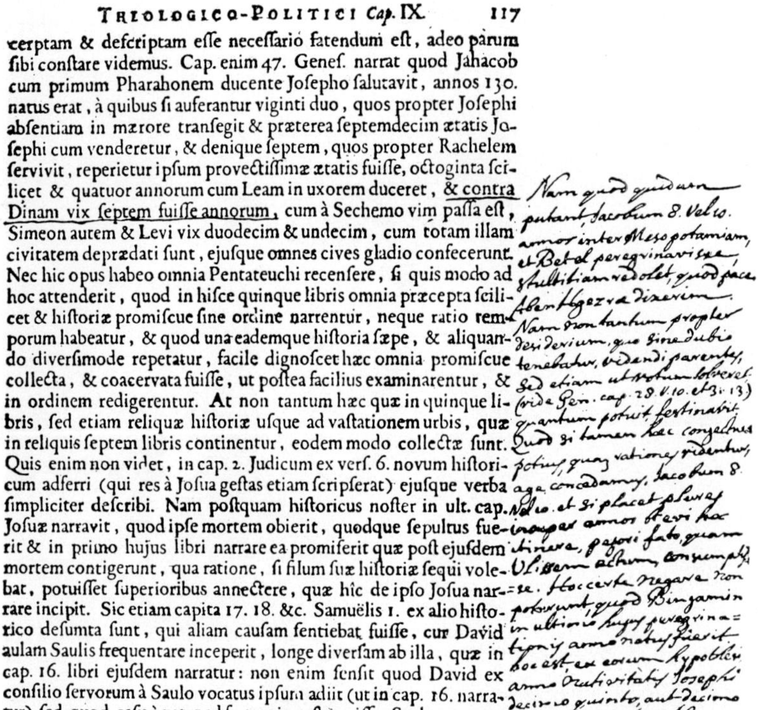
THEOLOGICO-POLITICI *Cap.* IX. 117

cerptam & descriptam esse necessario fatendum est, adeo parum sibi constare videmus. Cap. enim 47. Genes. narrat quod Jahacob cum primum Pharahonem ducente Josepho salutavit, annos 130. natus erat, à quibus si auferantur viginti duo, quos propter Josephi absentiam in mærore transegit & præterea septemdecim ætatis Josephi cum venderetur, & denique septem, quos propter Rachelem servivit, reperietur ipsum provectissimæ ætatis fuisse, octoginta scilicet & quatuor annorum cum Leam in uxorem duceret, & contra Dinam vix septem fuisse annorum, cum à Sechemo vim passa est, Simeon autem & Levi vix duodecim & undecim, cum totam illam civitatem deprædati sunt, ejusque omnes cives gladio confecerunt. Nec hic opus habeo omnia Pentateuchi recensere, si quis modo ad hoc attenderit, quod in hisce quinque libris omnia præcepta scilicet & historiæ promiscue sine ordine narrentur, neque ratio temporum habeatur, & quod una eademque historia sæpe, & aliquando diversimode repetatur, facile dignoscet hæc omnia promiscue collecta, & coacervata fuisse, ut postea facilius examinarentur, & in ordinem redigerentur. At non tantum hæc quæ in quinque libris, sed etiam reliquæ historiæ usque ad vastationem urbis, quæ in reliquis septem libris continentur, eodem modo collectæ sunt. Quis enim non videt, in cap. 2. Judicum ex vers. 6. novum historicum adferri (qui res à Josua gestas etiam scripserat) ejusque verba simpliciter describi. Nam postquam historicus noster in ult. cap. Josuæ narravit, quod ipse mortem obierit, quodque sepultus fuerit & in primo hujus libri narrare ea promiserit quæ post ejusdem mortem contigerunt, qua ratione, si filum suæ historiæ sequi volebat, potuisset superioribus annectere, quæ hîc de ipso Josua narrare incipit. Sic etiam capita 17. 18. &c. Samuëlis 1. ex alio historico desumta sunt, qui aliam causam sentiebat fuisse, cur David aulam Saulis frequentare inceperit, longe diversam ab illa, quæ in cap. 16. libri ejusdem narratur: non enim sensit quod David ex consilio servorum à Saulo vocatus ipsum adiit (ut in cap. 16. narratur) sed quod casu à patre ad fratres in castra missus Saulo ex occasione victoriæ, quam contra Philistæum Goliat habuit, tum demum innotuit, & in aula detentus fuit. Idem de cap. 26. ejusdem libri suspi-

P 3

Nam quod quidam putant Jacobum 8. vel 10. annos inter Mesopotamiam et Betel peregrinavisse, stultitiam redolet, quod pace Aben Hezra dixerim. Nam non tantum propter desiderium, quo sine dubio tenebatur, videndi parentes, sed etiam ut votum solveret (vide Gen. cap. 28. v. 10. et 31. 13) quantum potuit festinavit. Quod si tamen hæc conjecturæ potius, quam rationes videntur, Jacobum 8 æqe concedamus, Jacobum 8. vel 10. et si placet plures insuper annos brevi hoc itinere, pejori fato, quam Ulissem absumpsisse. Hoc certe negare non poterunt, quod Binjamin in ultimo hujus peregrinationis anno natus fuerit, hoc est ex eorum hypothesi anno nativitatis Josephi decimo quinto, aut decimo sexto, aut circiter. Nam Jacobus anno a nativitate ipsius Josephi septimo Labano valedixit. At ex anno 17° ætatis Josephi usque ad annum quo ipse patriarcha Egyptum peregravit non plures, quam viginti duo anni numerantur, ut in hoc ipso capite ostendimus, adeoque Binjamin eodem tempore, quo scil. Egyptum profectus est, viginti tres aut viginti quatuor annos ad summum habebat, quo ætatis flore nepotes eum habuisse constat (vide Gen. cap. 46. v. 21. quem confer cum v. 38. 39. 40. cap. 26. Num. et cum v. 1. et seq. cap. 8. l. 1. Paral.) quod sane non minus a ratione alienum est quam quod Dina septennis vim passa fuerit et reliqua quæ ex hujus historiæ ordine deduximus. atque adeo apparet homines imperitos, dum nodos solvere student in alios incidere, remque magis intricare, et dilacerare.

PLATE 22. Handwriting of Spinoza

PLATE 23. Rabbi Jonathan Eyebeschutz (1690-1764)
(Yaarat Devash)

PLATE 24. Rabbi Israel Baal Shem-Tov (1700-1760)
(Traditional portrait and signature)

PLATE 25. Rabbi Elijah of Wilna
(Ha-Cra 1720-1797)

PLATE 26. Moses Mendelssohn (1729-1786)

PLATE 27. David Friedlander (1750-1834)
Father of Reform Judaism

PLATE 28. Israel Jacobson (1768-1828), One of the Pioneers of Reform Judaism

(*The portrait is by Thomas Sully*)

PLATE 29. Rebecca Gratz (1781-1869), founder of the first Jewish Sunday School in the United States, and reported to be the prototype of Rebecca in Walter Scott's *Ivanhoe*.

PLATE 30. Leopold Zunz (1794-1886), Pioneer of Liberal Judaism and the Science of Judaism

PLATE 31. Zacharias Frankel (1801-1875), Father of Conservative Judaism

PLATE 32. Benjamin Disraeli (1804-1881)

Fichman, Jacob

(1881—)

Born in Bessarabia, this Hebrew poet is famed in Israel, his present home, and throughout the world.

Fig

Legendary forbidden fruit of Paradise.

First-born, Fast of

Because of sparing of Jewish first-born from tenth plague, later first-born sons are expected to fast the day before Passover.

Fiscus Judaicus

Humiliating tax imposed on all Jews in the Roman Empire after the destruction of the Temple in 70 C.E., and applied to the temple of Jupiter Capitolinus at Rome.

Fish

Kosher only with scales and fins; there are traditional fish dishes among observant Jews.

Flag, Jewish, Israeli

Designed by Herzl; white, with blue stripes, Star of David. White—symbol of priestly dress; blue—symbol of the heavens.

Forgiveness

The Jewish religion has always stressed two Divine attributes: Justice, which will not permit the guilty to escape, and Mercy in forgiving transgression and sin (Ex. 34:6-7). Since it is man's duty to follow in the footsteps of the Lord, he too must be guided by these ideals.

Franck, Adolphe

(1809-1893)

French philosopher, professor at the Sorbonne. His major work: *La Cabbale; ou Philosophie Réligieuse des Hébreux (The Cabbalah; or the Religious Philosophy of the Hebrews*).

Frank, Jacob

(1726-1791)

False Messiah, who gathered some of the followers of Shabbetai Zevi into a new messianic movement; he ultimately became a Catholic.

Frankel, Zacharias

(Prague, 1801–Breslau, 1875)

Took middle road in founding historical school of Jewish research; wrote Talmud and Bible studies and edited learned monthly.

Frankfurter, Aryeh Judah Lob

(17th-18th centuries)

Polish rabbi and Talmudist who printed and published a version of the Babylonian Talmud prepared by his father and other scholars.

Franzos, Karl Emil

(Podolia, 1848–Berlin, 1904)

Author of novels about East European Jewry and travel books (DIE JUDEN VON BARNOW, DER POIAZ, VOM DON ZUR DONAU).

Freud, Sigmund

(1856-1939)

Almost two decades ago he staggered the world in THE FUTURE OF AN ILLUSION with the charge that religion "is a universal, obsessional, neurosis of mankind," by means of which individuals are able to nurse themselves into an unhealthy state of immaturity. He contended that religion is an illusion due to be destroyed when mankind has overcome its infantile prejudices. God, in short, is nothing but a creation of man. Religion is a technique by means of which the person who is afraid of life tries to find a haven of false security. He reduced the idea of God to a rationalization of the father ideal and the infantile wish for protection from the terrors of nature. He departed from his lifelong analysis of unconscious motivations and attacked religion. He ignored the religious needs of men, and attacked the logic of theology which justifies these needs by arguing that science, the supremacy of intellect, can take its place. In his last work (*Moses and Monotheism*) he attempted to write a biography of the founder of the Hebrew nation, largely used as an occasion to work out and expand his well-known theory of religion. It was an ambitious construction resting on an extremely slight and tenuous foundation of historical data. Wishful speculation loomed large. In attacking religion unsparingly in his works, he was least astute here, and his polemics did him no credit. His discussion of religion showed a misunderstanding of what religion is, and he fell into a morass of inconsistencies. Notwithstanding Freud's eminent failure to understand the religious needs of men, he has done mankind a real service in ruthlessly exposing the unhealthy use of religion as a crutch. Freud regarded religion as mainly associated with human weakness; he was attacking the abuse rather than the use of religion. He never concerned himself with healthy religion. In fact, he did not know what normal, sane religion is.

Friedlaender, David

(1750-1834)

Pathfinder in German Reform Judaism.

Frishman, David

(Poland, 1860–Berlin, 1922)

Prolific Hebrew critic, editor, translator. (W) *Ophir, Tohu Wabohu.*

Frug, Simon S.

(1860-1916)

Poet in Russian and Yiddish languages; more distinguished in first.

Funeral customs

Anciently interment or encavement took place before sundown on day of death, generally without casket. Mourning songs by those close to deceased; sometimes professional mourners. Since 18th century, burial takes place up to three days after decease; the body washed, clad in shrouds (tachrichim), placed in plain coffin by local burial society, Chevra Kadisha ("Holy Society"). Tallis is buried with male. Prayers of comfort (Tzidduk ha-Din) precede burial; Kaddish follows. Cremation is generally frowned upon. These are traditional laws, not followed by many contemporary Jews. Other traditional customs opposed by liberals: cutting of garment by mourners, sitting seven (shivah) days of mourning with no toilette, omitting flowers.

Fuenn, Samuel Joseph

(1819-1891)

Russian historian, translator, lexicographer. Most important works: *Knesset Yisrael* (*The Community of Israel*), an encyclopedia of Jewish scholars, and *Haotzar* (*The Treasury*), a dictionary of Hebrew and Chaldean Biblical words.

Fuerst, Julius

(1805-1873)

German Hebraist and Orientalist, editor of the *Sabbathblatt,* author of *Bibliotheca Judaica* (*Bibliography of Jewish Literature*), a Hebrew and Aramaic dictionary, a history of Karaism, and a German edition of the Bible.

Funk, Solomon

(Hungary, 1867–Vienna, 1928)

Moravian rabbi and Talmudist, author of *Die Juden in Babylonien* (*The Jews in Babylon*).

Furtado, Abraham

(1756-1816)

A descendant of Portuguese Marranos, Furtado was a fighter for Jewish rights, president of Napoleon's Assembly of Jewish Notables in 1806, and a member of the conference of rabbis and Jewish laymen known as the Emperor's Sanhedrin (1807).

G

Gabbai

Once collector of taxes or synagogue funds, this official is now an honorary synagogue officer, such as stands by during the Torah reading.

Gabriel

Man of God; archangel; messenger of the Lord.

Gad

One of the twelve sons of Jacob, and so one of the twelve tribes of Israel. Also, as the name means "luck, fortune," a goddess. See ISAIAH 65:11 (R.V.).

Galach (Shaved)

A priest or monk; any Christian minister.

Galut

Exile; diaspora. First galut—10 lost tribes, 721 B.C.E., after Assyrian conquest. Babylonian galut, of Judah, 586. Roman galut, 70 C.E., after destruction of Second Temple.

Gam zu le-tovah

"This also is for good"—Talmudic support of faith in Providence; all is for the best.

Gamaliel I

Gamaliel I, also known as Gamaliel the Elder or Hazaken, a grandson of Hillel, was one of the most prominent and respected teachers of the Law of his day (30-60 C.E.) and occupied a leading position in the Sanhedrin, the highest court of Jerusalem. In fact, according to one tradition, he may have been the Nasi or head of the Sanhedrin. There are not many laws or opinions in the Talmud attributed to Gamaliel. However, a study of those recorded in his name shows that he was keenly aware of the needs of his day and did not hesitate to act boldly to meet them. One of the principles which guided him in many of his enactments was that law must lead to "improvement of the world" (*mippne tikkun ha'olam*) and promote the common good. Gamaliel is mentioned in Acts 5:34ff. as the Pharisee who favored leniency at the trial of the disciples, arguing that "if this work be of men, it will be overthrown (able to be); but if it is of God ye will not be able to overthrow them." Gamaliel is also mentioned in Acts 22:3, where Paul states that he was "brought up at the feet of Gamaliel."

Gamaliel II

First-century scholar, son of Simeon, grandson of Gamaliel I, himself grandson of Hillel. First called Prince (Nasi), he was a strong leader and disciplinarian, who led a deputation to Rome.

Gaon

(Excellency)

Reverential title of heads of Talmudic academies of Sura and Pumbedita, Babylonia. Rabbi Elijah of Wilna was accorded that title in the eighteenth century.

Gaster, Moses

(1856-1939)

Rumanian-born rabbi and scholar who became a teacher at Oxford, head of Sephardic Jews of England, leading world Zionist, author of historical, liturgical, and folklorist books, including *Samaritan Book of Joshua* and *Maaseh Book.*

Gedaliah

Governor of Judah after destruction of Jerusalem, 586 B.C.E. His assassination, compounding the country's hardships, is commemorated by a fast.

Gehenna

(Greek, "Geenna," from Hebrew, "Ge-Hinnom")

The valley of Hinnom, near Jerusalem, where early Israelites sacrificed children to Moloch; afterward regarded as a place of abomination and refuse, where fires continually burned to prevent pestilence.

Geiger, Abraham

(1810-1874)

Leader in German Reform movement, opposed by the Orthodox under Rabbi Solomon Tiktin. Prolific writer: *Judaism and Its History* and textual studies of the Bible.

Gelilah

Binding the Torah scroll after reading.

Gemara

The term Gemara is the Aramaic word for "learning," and as technically used is applied to the discussions of the rabbinic scholars on the Mishnah, the code of Jewish law, formulated by the famous Rabbi Judah I the Patriarch and his colleagues, early in the third century. This code became a text book in the Palestinian and Babylonian academies, where oral discussion of it, and comments on it, were crystallized into memorized books. These have come down to us in the form of the Palestinian Talmud and the Babylonian Talmud. The former originated in the academies of the Holy Land, in the third and fourth centuries: the latter in those of Babylonia in the third, fourth and fifth centuries. The Talmud includes both the Mishnah and the comments; the term Gemara is used exclusively for the comments.

Gematria

Finding meanings in the numerical value of Hebrew letters and words. See CABBALAH.

Gemilut Chasidim

Performance of deeds of kindness; welfare work.

General Zionists

Israel party, first founded 1922; conservative in its policies.

Genesis

The first book of the OT, being an account of the creation of the world and the primeval history of mankind (chapters 1-11) and the history of the patriarchs (chapters 12-50). Moses is considered the author by Jewish, Christian, and Islamic tradition, but the book is the product of a long process of writing and editing by J, E and P, reaching its final form ca. 400 B.C.E. Some scholars have claimed for the book other sources, such as S, an Edomite document (R. H. Pfeiffer) and L, a primitive lay source (Otto Eissenfeldt). In its present form Genesis shows a greater unity of conception and purpose than most of the other composite books of the Hexateuch. The first eleven chapters contain profound religious myths which resemble those of other civilizations of the ancient Near East; the story of the flood, for example, so closely resembles the account of the flood in the Gilgamesh Epic as to suggest direct or ultimate dependence upon it. The remainder of Genesis consists of legends concerning the patriarchs, the fathers of the Hebrew nation. Recent archaeological discoveries, especially at Nuzi in northern Mesopotamia, tend to authenticate the general background of these legends, but their historicity in detail cannot be affirmed.

Genizah

Place of concealment for disused scrolls and books containing holy tongue. Solomon Schechter discovered most famed Genizah in Cairo synagogue.

Ger ("Stranger")

Convert to Judaism. He is to be received with special kindness. Rabbi Akiba was of non-Jewish descent. The Talmud tells of a variety of *gerim*: the ger of love; of the king's table (opportunists); of the lion (fear); of the dream (persuaded by dream or omen); there are also "tramp" converts and the convert of true conviction—*ger tzedek.*

Gershom ben Judah of Mayence

(960-1040)

Known as Rabbenu Gershom and Meor ha-Golah (Light of the Exile), the head of the Mayence academy prohibited polygamy among Jews and divorce without wife's consent.

Gersonides

(1288-1344)

Levi ben Gershom, called Gersonides, was the greatest astronomer of his time. His writings attracted the interest of Kepler and his inventions, the "Jacob's staff" to measure visual angles and the *camera obscura,* became of great use. He also wrote on physics, physiology, mathematics, logic, ethics, psychology, metaphysics, the Bible and Talmud. Whatever he dealt with, he did so in a new manner. In some regards he was a precursor of Galileo, in others even of modern thinkers like Bertrand Russell, for Gersonides' principal problem in general philosophy was the relation between individual experience and the body of scientific knowledge, or the way science can be developed and subsist in the course of history. As a philosopher of religion, Gersonides, in his principal work *Milhamoth Adonai* (*The Wars of the Lord*), made a vigorous effort to integrate the historical experience of the Jewish people into a conception of the universe that rests upon the secular sciences of astronomy, physics and the other branches with which he was acquainted. He insisted that scientific research must be conducted independently of the Torah, which, he said, does not compel men to believe what is not true. But he was convinced that truth, in accordance with modern science, is contained in the Torah, though not explicitly, and that the history of the Jewish people reflects and confirms the universal truth, in whose discovery time plays an important part. A large part of Gersonides' writings is either lost or still unpublished.

Get

Aramaic word for Jewish ritual divorce.

Geullah

Redemption; liturgical section between Shema and Tefillah (Amidah) is so named.

Gezerah

Rabbinical decree.

Ghetto

Restricted sections in which Jews were forced to live. In antiquity, in Rome and Alexandria; in medieval times, in Europe, until the emancipation. Generally in least desirable section of city (Frankfurt-am-Main, near garbage dump). Overcrowding in walled ghettoes sometimes compelled burials five deep.

Gideon

One of the prominent judges of Israel who defeated the Midianites in battle.

Gikatilla, Joseph
(1248-1305)

Spanish Talmudist and Cabbalist; author of many mystic works and commentaries.

Ginzberg, Asher
(Ukraine, 1856-Tel Aviv, 1927)

Best known under his pseudonym, Achad Ha-Am ("One of the People"), Ginzberg became noted as a philosopher and contributor to the revival of the Hebrew language and Hebrew literature. He also played a significant role in the modern Jewish nationalist movement. Although his writings deal principally with Jewish affairs, his fundamental ideas are of general interest. Dissatisfied with material evolution, he emphasized the importance of spiritual evolution. He concentrated upon the moral aspects of all problems, rejecting that relationship between ethics and religion where the role of ethics is limited only to the confines of a sociological frame of reference. He regarded ethics as the most important determinant in national character and, for that reason, insisted that the national development of ethical views precedes all political activity. His aim was to harmonize nationalistic sentiments with the necessary sense of responsibility for the future of human civilization. The success of that aim will depend on one's devotion to the ideals of justice enunciated by the prophets of the Old Testament. His concept of Zionism established him as a genuine philosopher. It is founded upon an original explanation of reality and ideals. For many years he was opposed to political Zionism, advocating, instead, the establishment of a Jewish cultural center in Palestine. This, he hoped, would become a "center of emulation" for Jews dispersed all over the world, effectively raising their cultural standards, and inspiring them to produce a genuine Jewish culture. Principal Work: *Al Parashat Derachim* (*At the Crossroads*).

Gladiator

Reference to Rabbi Simeon ben Lakish (third century), who was a gladiator before engaging in study and teaching of Talmud.

Glycenstein, Henryk

(1850-1942)

Polish etcher, sculptor, and painter; died in U.S.

Gobineau, Joseph Arthur

(1816-1882)

French founder of pseudoscientific race theories, arrogantly denouncing the Semites.

God

Among the almost hundred synonyms for God in Biblical and rabbinical literature are Father of Mercy; Lord, the One, Eternal, Truth, Creator, Destroyer (Shaddai), Judge, Eye of the World, King of Kings, Holy One, the Name, Heaven, and Man (whence the Christian Son of Man).

Goel ha-Dam

Avenger of the blood; closest relative of murdered person, bound to avenge him. Palestinian "cities of refuge" were provided for security of unintentional killers.

Gog and Magog

Enigmatic names occurring in Ezekiel's apocalyptic vision of the final assault of the fierce armed hordes of the North on the land of Israel prior to the inauguration of God's sovereignty (Ezek. 38-39). While Josephus identifies them with the Scythians (Ant. I, 6:1), the Sybilline Oracles III, 319, places them in Ethiopia. In rabbinic literature they figure as the rebel peoples who rise up against God and His anointed (Midr. Psalms, ed. Buber, 2,2; Ber. 7b; cf. Revel. 20:8).

Goldfaden, Abraham

(Volhynia, 1840–New York, 1908)

Folk poet and founder of Yiddish theater. His plays are Yiddish classics, including *Bar Kokhba, Shulamit,* and *Schmendrik.*

Golem

See JUDAH LOEW BEN BEZALEEL.

Gordin, Jacob

(Ukraine, 1853–New York, 1909)

Radical Yiddish playwright—Russia and U.S. (W) *Kreutzer Sonata, Yetomoh, Miracle Effros, Shechita, Sappho, Gott, Mensch un Taiwel.*

Gordon, Aaron David

(1856-1922)

Russian-Palestinian philosopher of the Chalutz movement.

Goy

Hebrew for "a people." Now the word is used to mean gentile.

Graetz, Heinrich

(1817-1891)

German Jewish historian who wrote monumental history of the Jews.

Gratz, Rebecca

(1781-1869)

Philadelphia citizen who established first Jewish Sunday School there, and other welfare organizations; reputed original of character in *Ivanhoe.*

Great Assembly, Men of (Knesset ha-Gedolah)

Palestine legislative body at time of Second Temple.

Great Sabbath

(Shabbat ha-Gadol)

The Sabbath preceding Passover.

Great Synagogue, The

The Great Synagogue, also known as the Great Assembly, refers to the group of scholars who met from time to time, beginning during the days of Ezra and continuing for two centuries after him, to interpret existing laws and to enact new ordinances. The exact nature of this group, their number and internal organization, are somewhat obscure. Later generations, however, ascribed many important institutions to this body, from which we may infer that it was very active and was regarded as authoritative.

H

Habakkuk

A lengthy poem on the fall of Babylon, with minor interpolations in chapters 1-2. Chapter 3 consists wholly of later appended psalm materials. Although usually dated 612-586 B.C.E., it appears more likely Habakkuk was an exile, writing his poem between 455 and 445, as it began to appear that Persia might be able to conquer Babylonia. After reviewing the past depredations of Babylon, he asked God how soon would be the overthrow, receiving assurance it would be sure and soon. The poem ends with heaping woes upon Babylon. The distinctive prophetic ethics, religion, and reforming genius are absent. Like Nahum, Habakkuk was more distinctly a poet. His was an outburst of indignation against Babylonia, which had brought the Judeans into bondage.

Haboker

Organ of the General Zionist party in Israel.

Habonim

Pioneer Youth Zionist organization.

Hachsharah (Training)

Preparatory agricultural and trade education for chalutzim (Israeli pioneers).

Hadassah

American Zionist Women's Organization, founded by Henrietta Szold in 1912, concentrating on medical and nursing welfare work in Israel. (Hadassah-myrtle, part of festival bouquet on Sukkoth.)

Hadlakat Nerot

Kindling the candles, by housewife.

Haftarah

Appropriate and supplementary reading from the Prophets, recited after Torah portions on Sabbaths and festivals.

Haganah

"Defense" group of Palestinian settlers, later incorporated into Army of Israel; defended new state.

Hagbahah

Lifting the Torah scroll at end of reading.

Haggadah

(Also Agada or Aggadah)

A general Hebrew term for utterance, applied specifically to the nonlegal portion of rabbinic literature. It is also the title of the text recited at the festive meal (seder) on the first two nights of Passover.

Haggai

First postexilic prophetic book, with record of four addresses to the returned exiles at Jerusalem between August and December, 520 B.C.E. The eighteen-year-old community had become discouraged by crop failures, drought, and hostility of neighbors until they were ready to return to Babylon. Haggai reprimanded them for leaving the Temple unbuilt. After they started a small structure, Haggai spoke again, calling the people to build even more gloriously than Solomon. He also planned to restore the monarchy with Zerubbabel as king. Very different from reforming pre-exilic prophets, Haggai was more priestly, stressing temple worship and ritual as the key to prosperity.

Hagiographa

(Greek, *hagios*, "sacred"; *grapho*, "I write")

The Sacred Writings, an alternative designation of Christian origin for the books of the third division of the Hebrew canon of scripture, viz., all books other than those of the Law and the Prophets. This is known to Jews as The Writings (Ketuvim).

Hai ben Sherira Gaon

(939-1038)

Last of the geonim of Babylonia; head of Pumbedita academy; codifier, commentator, lexicographer; recognized as authority by world Jewry, as attested by many extant responsa. Author of *Dictionary of Difficult Words in Talmud, Torah and Targum.*

Hakafah (Circuit)

Synagogue procession, on Hoshanah Rabbah with the prescribed Sukkoth vegetation, and on Simchat Torah with the Torah scrolls.

Hakhnassat Orchim

Hospitality.

Halakhah

The way one goes; the word for law, or for the purely legal and regulatory portions of the Talmud, and of all Jewish lore.

Halakhah l'Mosheh MiSinai

A law ascribed back to Moses on Sinai.

Halevai

Aramaic: "Would that . . ."

Halevi, Judah

(About 1085-1140)

As a "flaming pillar of song," Judah Halevi, the greatest Jewish poet of the Middle Ages, was exalted by Heinrich Heine, who, himself an undeniable expert, sensed through the medium of a translation Halevi's mastership of versification and his fervent soul. Halevi sang of love and friendship, of virtue and beauty, and most passionately of the fate of the Jewish people, of Zion and God. Several of his sacred poems form part of Jewish prayer books in every country where Jewish congregations exist. But Halevi was also an important philosopher of religion. His *Kitab Al Khazari,* written in Arabic and translated into Hebrew under the title *Sefer Ha-Kuzari* (*Book of the Khazar*), referring to the conversion to Judaism of the Khazar King Bulan II (about 740), is a defense of the Jewish faith against Christian and Islamic attacks and at the same time, a profound meditation on Jewish history and an acute demarcation between philosophy and religion. The close connection between the revealed religion and the history of the Jewish people is characteristic of Halevi's position. He maintained that Judaism does not center in the person of its founder as the religions of Christ and Mohammed do but in the people to whom the Torah has been given, and he goes so far as to declare: "If there were no Jews there would be no Torah." But he by no means idolizes his people in the way modern nationalists do. Jewish history is the work of Divine Providence which he regarded as the continuation of the Divine creative activity. Halevi was opposed to Aristotelianism which he reproached for subjecting the Deity to necessity and for being incompatible with the idea of a personal God. Platonic tradition seemed more fitting to him, for he was inclined to regard God as the principle of form that molds the eternal material principle. Fundamentally, however, Halevi remained reluctant to use philosophical categories in matters that concern religion, and he often expressed his dislike of philosophy and philosophers, although he proved to be one of them.

Halkin, Simon

(1899—)

Russian-American poet and critic now living in Israel; wrote *Hebrew Literature in Palestine*; *Modern Hebrew Literature.*

Hallel ("Praise")

Designation of Psalms 113-118; included in the Jewish liturgy for

New Moon and the festivals of Tabernacles, Chanukah, Pentecost, and in the Passover service.

Hallelujah ("Praise ye the Lord")

Frequent interjection (like "Amen") in the Psalms.

Haman

Legendary archenemy of the Jews. Favorite of Ahasuerus (Xerxes), fifth century B.C.E. Ends up on gallows. Central figure of Purim story. Customs: burning of Haman dolls; Hamantaschen (Haman pockets), filled triangular Purim cakes.

Hamann, Johann Georg (1730-1788)

During a stay in London, where he was bound to become acquainted with British business methods, Hamann, a native of Königsberg, Prussia, had a mystical experience which made him a grim adversary of rationalism and the spirit of enlightenment that fascinated most of his contemporaries. With the aid of allegorical interpretation, Hamann regarded the Bible as the fundamental book of all possible knowledge, including that of nature. Allegory and symbol gave Hamann truer knowledge than abstractions. Myths and poetry were to him of greater validity than scientific research and logical conclusions. Language was the key that opens the door to reality. Hamann was a past master in sensing the unconscious tendencies of speech. But in his style there are no consequences, no development of ideas. He tried to grasp the flux of life, but, according to his own avowal, often forgot the meaning of the similes he had used and to which he alluded in later pages of the same treatise. His fugitive associations, therefore, are of greater value than his efforts to express his intentions elaborately. Devout and coquettish, excessive in his piety and repentance of transgressions with which his imagination remained fascinated, Hamann tried to embrace spirit and sensuality, sometimes illuminating their relations, sometimes becoming hopelessly confused.

His writings were inspired by sublime earnestness and brilliant irony. He accused the rationalistic spirit of his age of ignoring God and nature, human genius, creative action and the enjoyment of real life. His views deeply impressed Herder, Goethe, Friedrich Heinrich Jacobi, Hegel and Kierkegaard.

Hanaah

Pleasure; satisfaction.

Hannah

Mother of prophet Samuel. Because of her whispered prayers at the Tabernacle for a son, some prayers are still recited in that memory in a low voice.

Hapoel Hamizrachi

Religious workers' party in Israel and the world, now part of Religious Zionist Organization.

Hasideans

Pietists; supporters of Judas Maccabeus; urging ritual observance and faith, they were precursors of the Pharisees.

Haskalah

(Enlightenment)

The eighteenth century movement designed to modernize the Jew and his culture. Though Mendelssohn and other faithful Jews supported the movement, it degenerated into a trend toward assimilation.

Haskamah

Corroboration; sanction. Book publishing license since late middle ages, to prevent public offense.

Hasmoneans (also Asmoneans)

The dynasty commencing with Simon, brother of Judas Maccabeus, deliverer of the Jewish people from the oppressive Syrian yoke, who became king of the Jews in 142 B.C.E., and ending with Antigonus, executed by Mark Antony 37 B.C.E. These successive rulers combined in their persons the offices of the king and high priest. Herod the Great, an Idumean, became king by marrying Mariamne, the last Hasmonean princess.

Hatikvah

Zionist, and now Israel national anthem, composed by N. H. Imber.

Hatzofeh

Organ of the United Religious Zionists party in Israel.

Havdalah (Separation)

Blessing over wine, spices, and lights at close of Sabbath, or over wine and spices, or wine alone, at conclusion of festivals. Special braided candles are used; and the spices are placed in an ornate container. A savory odor may help drive off unpleasant thoughts when holy day departs.

Haycraft Commission

In 1921 investigated the causes of Arab-Jewish differences for the British Parliament.

Hazzaz, Chaim

(Russia, 1898——)

Israeli writer, fictionist, on Russian and Oriental Jewish life.

Hazmanah

Summons; invitation.

Hebrew

The word may mean one who "crosses" from the other side of the Euphrates, a trespasser, a nomad, or a descendant of Eber, himself descended from Shem. The language, with 22 letters, and vowels added by the Masoretes, is that of the Bible, with some exceptions in Aramaic, the tongue that became the everyday language of the Jews after the Babylonian exile. Hebrew, however, was the language of prayer and sanctity; the Mishnah is written in Hebrew. New Testament references to Aramaic as the Hebrew tongue are erroneous.

Hebrew language

Ancient tongue in which most of the OT was written. Transformed and used in rabbinic literature, today revived by the Zionists. Belongs to the Northwestern branch of the Semitic family. Characterized by its consonantal stability, the triliterality of the radicals, its wide use of prefixes and suffixes, of nominal construct states, the flexibility of its verbal voice-system, and the simplicity of its syntax. Offers concise and forceful means of expression, especially for epic and lyric poetry.

Hebrew Union College—Jewish Institute of Religion

Reform seminary founded by Isaac M. Wise in Cincinnati, 1875. The College, oldest Jewish seminary in America, was combined in 1950 with the Institute, founded 1922 in New York by Stephen S. Wise.

Hebron

Ancient city of Southern Palestine, 19 miles south of Jerusalem, formerly called Kiriath-Arba (Jud.I: 10-15); first capital of David (II Sam. 2:4, etc.).

Hechal ha-Kodesh

Hebrew Bible concordance by Solomon Mandelkern (1896).

Hechalutz

Organization for training Israeli colonizers.

Hechasid, Judah ben Samuel of Regensburg

(12th and 13th centuries)

The Hebrew word *Hehasid* means "the Saint." Judah's coreligionists revered him because he was an extremely pious man, absorbed in mystical contemplation, a great teacher, scholar and a careful leader of the Jewish community of Regensburg where he settled in 1195. He was the initiator of Jewish mysticism in Germany, a way of thinking and feeling that is different from cabbalistic mysticism because it insists more on prayer and moral conduct. Judah denied all possibility of human understanding of God. Man must fulfill his religious duties, as they are prescribed in the Bible. Without reasonable knowledge of the Almighty, but, by purification, obedience to ceremonial life and asceticism, he may obtain union with God that is beyond reasoning. In this way, Judah tried to reconcile the demands of orthodox Judaism with enjoyment of mystical ecstasy. Judah's biography is adorned with many legends which testify to the admiration of his contemporaries and succeeding generations. He wrote *Sefer Hasidim* (*Book of the Pious*), and *Sefer Hakavod* (*Book of Glory*). The second book has been lost. It is known only by quotations other authors have made from it.

Heine, Heinrich

(Germany, 1797-1856)

Greatest lyricist in the German tongue. Regarded as leader of Young Germany. Settled in Paris, and interpreted French and Germans to each other. A hasty convert who remained a tender admirer of Judaism and acid critic of Christianity all his life. Noted for his irony, wit, mercurial intelligence. Famous poems: "*Die Lorelei*," "*Du Bist Wie eine Blume*." (W) *Book of Songs*, *Romanzero*, *Travel Pictures*.

Hekdesh

Things dedicated to Temple or sacrifice use.

Hekesh

Derivation of law by inference and analogy.

Hekhal

Temple hall containing the golden altar. Also, container of Torah scrolls.

Hellenism

A term used to describe ancient Greek culture. After the time of Alexander the Great the Greek speech and manner of thinking pervaded the lands around the eastern end of the Mediterranean Sea, and thus there arose a cultural development termed Hellenistic in contrast with the original Hellenic civilization of Greece itself. In English the noun "Hellenism" may refer to either of these phases of Greek culture, but it is the Hellenistic rather than the Hellenic that is of greatest significance for Judaism in the Dispersion and for early Christianity on gentile soil.

Heretic

Completely rejected by Judaism only when he seeks to destroy his people's faith. Unlike a frequently expressed notion, the Jewish faith allows for wide divergence in theologic interpretation; the greater stress has always been on practical observances. Even the agnostic is still considered a Jew, though not a good one.

Herod

(37-4 B.C.E.)

Half-Jewish; last independent ruler of a Jewish kingdom.

Herut Movement

Israel party, opposed to the present regime in Israel and calling for the territorial integrity of Eretz Israel within its historic boundaries on both sides of the Jordan.

Herzl, Theodor

(1860-1904)

Austrian journalist who, under stimulus of the Dreyfus Case, became chief architect of modern Zionism. Reburied in Israel.

Hesped

Funeral oration.

Hess, Moses

(1812-1875)

Hess, who assumed the first name Moses instead of Moritz in order to show his adherence to Judaism, provoked the indignation of his relatives by marrying a prostitute in order to show his contempt of the existing moral standards. He lived with her in happiness until his death. He was, however, a man who willingly obeyed those ethical demands that his thinking recognized as right. He was an early apostle of socialism, and a precursor of Zionism. Because of his participation in the revolution of 1848, Hess was sentenced to death and on escaping had to wander through many countries of Europe before he found refuge in Paris.

In his youth, Hess abounded in ideas. His influence with Karl Marx was considerable. For a time they were closely associated. Later Marx felt himself superior to Hess, and made him smart for his previous ascendancy. Although Hess recognized the importance of economic and social forces, he conceived socialism as a prevalently humanitarian ideal, dissenting from Marx who regarded it as the inevitable result of economic evolution. It was also for the sake of humanity that Hess agitated for the establishment of a Jewish commonwealth in Palestine by publishing his book *Rome and Jerusalem* (1862) and numerous essays in which he expresses messianic hopes. According to Hess, Judaism has no other dogma but "the teaching of the unity." As already shown by his *Holy Story of Humanity* (1837), he deviated from the Jewish conception of God and called the history of humanity holy because, in his opinion, it is really the history of God, then conceived by him partly in accordance with Spinoza, partly the Christian doctrine of Trinity. In *European Triarchy* (1841) he outlined a new order of Europe which he claimed was in accordance with "human nature." His socialism is not strictly egalitarian but an effort to satisfy the wants of "human nature," which remained his principal standard of judging human institutions. In his later years he came closer to the views developed in Jewish traditions but he built his hopes for the settlement of the Jews in the Holy Land upon France, which he regarded as the champion of liberty. After France's defeat in the war of 1870, he admonished the nations of Europe to ally with one another against German militarism.

Hexateuch (Six Books)

Pentateuch plus Book of Joshua.

HIAS

Hebrew Sheltering and Immigrant Aid Society, formed in 1898 to assist immigrants in the Americas; its activities have extended to all parts of the world.

High place

(Semitic place of worship)

"High place" is the translation

of the Hebrew word "bamah," which signifies both elevation and sanctuary, in accordance with the Semitic and particularly Canaanitic custom of establishing sanctuaries at high points. The connection of divinity with mountains is found in all parts of the Near East, especially in Syria and Asia Minor. Not all bamot, however, were on hills, e.g. that of Gezar. They were sometimes in valleys, open air shrines marked by "mazzebot" (stone pillars) and "asherah" (sacred wooden post), lavers, images of the gods, and other cultic objects. In such cases the word "bamah" seems to refer to the elevated structure of the shrine itself, and this may well be the original meaning of the word. These bamot were not exclusively Canaanitic. YHWH, God of Israel, also had His legitimate bamot. The corrupt influences of foreign idolatry, however, rendered the continued existence of bamot in Israel and Judea a distinct danger to the holiness of YHWH and to national survival, and the Prophets denounced them in the strongest terms. Several attempts were made, as a result, by Judean kings to root out the bamot, the best known under Josiah (2 Kings 22:3; 2 Chron. 34:3).

High Priest

The highest ecclesiastical official in the Jewish priestly organization in Biblical literature. Biblical tradition represented him as being a descendant of Aaron; this is, however, historically untrue. Actually all passages in the Bible which refer to the high priest date from the last quarter of the fifth century B.C.E. or even later. The office itself was instituted only in 411 B.C.E. The high priest was the chief ecclesiastical ministrant in the Temple at Jerusalem at the most important religious festivals and functions in the Jewish calendar, and especially in the momentous ceremonies of the annual Day of Atonement. He likewise presided over the Sanhedrin. The office came to an end with the destruction of the Temple by the Romans in 70 C.E.

Hillel

Hillel I, also known as Hillel the Elder (Ha-Zaken), was the most prominent Jewish teacher of the first century (30 B.C.E.-10 C.E.), founder of an influential school which bears his name (Beth Hillel), and ancestor of the patriarch leaders of Palestinian Jewry during the first four centuries of the common era. A Babylonian by birth and, according to tradition, of Davidic stock, Hillel migrated (in early manhood) to Palestine to sit at the feet of the great masters of Biblical interpretation and exposition, Shemaiah and Abtalion. Despite great poverty and hardship (cf. Yoma 35b) Hillel pursued his studies with rare diligence and zeal, and rapidly became one of the keenest masters of the Bible. Such was his fame that when the Bene Bathyra, the heads of the college, resigned, Hillel was appointed to succeed them and became the recognized authority among scholars of the Law. Later generations are indebted to him for the formulation of seven rules for the systematic exposition of the Bible. These rules became basic for later rabbinic reasoning. Hillel is revered not only for his profound scholarship but also for his inspiring saintliness. Humility and love for his fellow men are the keystones of his character. All the legends which later generations wove about him as well as the sayings ascribed to him reveal these two traits. Perhaps the best appreciation of his character can be gained from the story of the heathen who came to Hillel and asked for a concise statement of the essence of Judaism. Hillel replied, "What is hateful to thee, do not unto thy fellow men; this is the whole Law; the rest is mere commentary" (Shab. 31a).

Hillel II

(320-365 C.E.)

Palestinian patriarch and scholar. In 344 established permanent Jewish calendar.

Hillel Foundation

Bnai Brith organization to

proliferate Jewish life and study in American institutions of learning.

Hillel of Verona

(1220-1295)

Physician and philosopher.

Hirsch, Emil Gustav

(Luxemburg, 1852-Chicago, 1923)

Outstanding Reform rabbi and orator.

Hirsch, Baron Maurice de

(1831-1896)

European banker, statesman, philanthropist, who gave millions to Jewish educational (trades and agriculture) causes, and colonization efforts. A fund in his name operates in the United States.

Hirsch, Samson Raphael

(1808-1888)

Leader of neo-Orthodoxy in Germany. Wrote *19 Letters of Ben Uzziel, Israel's Duties in the Diaspora,* and lengthy Bible commentaries and liturgical works.

Histadruth

Short for Histadruth ha-Ovdim, Workers' Union, founded 1920, and now most powerful group of unionists and employers in Israel; basis of the dominant Mapai (Socialist) party.

Histadrut Ivrit

American cultural organization that publishes Hebrew books and periodicals.

Hitlahavut

(Chasidic) ecstasy or God-intoxication.

Hittites

Frequently mentioned along with Canaanites in Bible, their empire was destroyed by the Egyptians.

Hiyya, Abraham Bar

(about 1065-1136)

While Christianity and Islam

met each other on the battlefield, Abraham bar Hiyya, called by his fellow Jews "the prince," and by non-Jews "Savasorda" (Latinization of his Arabic title, Sahib al Shurta, "governor of a city"), took a leading part in promoting spiritual interchange between the representatives of the Christian and Arabic civilizations, without neglecting his principal task, namely the vindication of the Jewish faith and its harmonization with science and philosophy. His treatise on areas and measurements which introduced new scientific terms and methods for the measurement of surfaces, was translated into Latin under the title *Liber Embadorum,* and for centuries, it remained a standard work. His contributions to mathematics, astronomy, music and optics were highly appreciated by Jewish, Christian and Moslem scholars. In his *Hegyon Hanefesh* (*Reflection on the soul*), Abraham bar Hiyya, while exposing his ideas on creation and the destiny and conduct of man, showed a strong inclination to the ascetic conception of life.

Hofjude (Court Jew)

Class of Jews whose financial and other services won them special privileges from rulers until the French Revolution.

Holdheim, Samuel

(1806-1860)

Leader of extreme German Reform movement.

Holiday Eves

Jewish holy days begin at nightfall, as indicated by phrase, "It was evening and it was morning," in Genesis.

Holiday Revision

Liberal Jews defend riding to services on Sabbath because of distances in modern life; attending to business on Saturday if necessary, because of complicated modern social structure (newspapers, telephone, elevator; reduction of extra day of holidays, originally added out of fear of error in calculating calendar in diaspora)—on ground that worship hallows Sabbath, not restrictions.

Holy Days

HOLIDAYS and FASTS	5719–תשי״ט 1958	5720–תש״כ 1959	5721–תשכ״א 1960	5722–תשכ״ב 1961	5723–תשכ״ג 1962
Rosh Hashanah . . .	Sept. 15-16	Oct. 3-4	Sept. 22-23	Sept. 11-12	Sept. 29-30
Fast of Gedaliah . . .	Sept. 17	Oct. 5	Sept. 25	Sept. 13	Oct. 1
Yom Kippur	Sept. 24	Oct. 12	Oct. 1	Sept. 20	Oct. 8
Sukkoth	Sept. 29-4	Oct. 17-22	Oct. 6-11	Sept. 25-30	Oct. 13-18
Hoshana Rabah . . .	Oct. 5	Oct. 23	Oct. 12	Oct. 1	Oct. 19
Shemini Atzereth . .	Oct. 6	Oct. 24	Oct. 13	Oct. 2	Oct. 20
Simchath Torah . . .	Oct. 7	Oct. 25	Oct. 14	Oct. 3	Oct. 21
Hanukkah	Dec. 7-14	Dec. 26-2	Dec. 14-21	Dec. 3-10	Dec. 22-29
		1960			1963
Fast of 10th of Teveth .	Dec. 21	January 10	Dec. 29	Dec. 17	Jan. 6
	1959		1961	1962	
Fast of Esther	Mar. 23	March 10	Mar. 1	March 19	March 7
Purim	Mar. 24	March 13	Mar. 2	March 20	March 10
Pesach (Passover) . .	Apr. 23-30	April 12-19	Apr. 1-8	April 19-26	April 9-16
Shavuoth	June 12-13	June 1-2	May 21-22	June 8-9	May 29-30
Fast of 17th of Tamuz	July 23	July 12	July 2	July 19	July 9
Fast of 9th of Av . . .	Aug. 13	August 2	July 23	August 9	July 30

There are several fast days in addition to Tishah B'Av. The second days of festivals, not observed in Israel, are also not observed by liberal Jews everywhere.

Holy of Holies (Kodesh Kadashim)

The most sacred chamber of the Tabernacle and then the Temple, where the high priest performed the Day of Atonement ritual. The Ark of the Covenant was kept there. The exact measurements of the Holy of Holies in the Temple of Solomon are described in I Kings 6.

Holy Place

A site held sacred because of its religious associations. The principal holy place in Judaism is the site on which formerly stood the Temple in Jerusalem, with the portion of wall which still survives and which is known as the Wailing Wall. It is a popular place for Jewish pilgrims who would weep there for the tragedies of the Jewish dispersion.

Home

True center of Jewish religious life. One reason that Judaism survived where synagogues were closed and assembly made difficult.

Homeland

Applied to the Land of Israel. First name, in antiquity, Canaan; later, Palestine. Chronology of the Zionist movement for regaining the land: 1897, first Zionist Congress, Basle; 1917, Balfour Declaration; 1920, League of Nations mandate to Britain, effective 1923; 1922, U.S. Congress approves Declaration; 1939, Great Britain offers independence in ten years to both Jews and Arabs; 1947, U.N. Assembly creates commission to study Palestine problem; May 14, 1948, State of Israel proclaimed, U.S. recognition; 1949, Israel admitted to U.N.

Horns

Shown on Moses in European art. The same Hebrew word means "horn" or "ray of light." Error may be from Latin Bible, through confusion between *cornuta* (horned) and *coronata* (crowned).

Hosanna ("O save!")

Liturgical cry of invocation during Sukkoth procession.

Hosea

First of Minor Prophets, 750 B.C.E., who compared Israel's unfaithfulness to God to marital infidelity.

Hoshaanot

Prayers for salvation during Sukkoth.

Hoshanah Rabbah

This is the "great" prayer for help, the seventh day of Sukkoth, a half-holiday on which there are a procession and special chants in the synagogue.

Hoshea

King of Israel in 722 B.C.E. when the Assyrians overcame the kingdom and took the inhabitants captive.

House of Life (Bet Chaim)

Euphemism for cemetery.

Hulda

Prophetess during period of First Temple.

Hunting

Jewish law forbids hunting of animals. They must be slaughtered only in a specified painless manner.

Hyksos

An ancient people (Hittites?) that conquered Egypt (seventeenth and sixteenth centuries B.C.E.) under the "shepherd kings." By some hypothesized as Hebrews.

Hyrcanus

Greek name of two Hasmoneans.

I

Ibn Abitur, Joseph

Spanish Jewish poet and Talmudist, 1000.

Ibn Daud, Abraham

(1110-1180)

Spanish historian, philosopher, scientist. Wrote *Sefer ha-Kabbalah* (*Book of Tradition*) against Karaism; and *Emunah Ramah* (*Lofty Faith*), a partial harmonization of Judaism and Aristotelianism.

Ibn Ezra, Abraham

(Spanish-Hebrew, 1092-1167)

Wandering hymnist and philosopher. Traveled through many non-Moslem lands, so became first Hebrew-Spaniard to write entirely in Hebrew. Wrote many liturgical poems, philosophic works, and an Arabic study of Spanish-Hebrew poetry. (W) *Yesod Mora* (*Foundation of Reverence*).

Ibn Ezra, Moses

(1070-1138)

Rhetorician, philosopher, and outstanding poet of Spanish period.

Ibn Gabirol, Solomon

(About 1021–about 1058)

From the middle of the twelfth to the end of the fourteenth century, Dominicans and Franciscans struggled with great bit-

PLATE 33. Samson Raphael Hirsch (1808-1888), Leading Orthodox Rabbi of 19th Century Germany

PLATE 34. Abraham Geiger (1810-1874), Eminent Representative of Reform Judaism

PLATE 35. Moses Hess (1812-1875)

PLATE 36. Isaac M. Wise (1819-1900)

PLATE 37. Emma Lazarus (1849-1887) in 1872

(Courtesy of Jewish Theological Seminary of America)

PLATE 38. Solomon Schechter (1850-1915)

PLATE 39. Achad-Haam
(Asher Ginzberg 1856-1927)

PLATE 40. Sholem Aleichem (1859-1916)

(*Courtesy Musaf Lakore Hatzair,* Hadoar Weekly)

PLATE 41. Rabbi Abraham Isaac Kook (1865-1935)

PLATE 42. Nathan Birnbaum

(*Zionist Archives and Library of the Palestine Foundation Fund*)

PLATE 43. Stephen S. Wise

(*Zionist Archives and Library of the Palestine Foundation Fund*)

PLATE 44. Chaim Weizmann

(*Zionist Archives and Library of the Palestine Foundation Fund*)

PLATE 45. Abba Hillel Silver

(Zionist Archives and Library of the Palestine Foundation Fund)

PLATE 46. David Ben-Gurion

(Zionist Archives and Library of the Palestine Foundation Fund)

PLATE 47. Nahum Goldmann

(Zionist Archives and Library of the Palestine Foundation Fund)

PLATE 48. Sir Herbert Samuel

terness over the ideas expressed in the book *Fons Vitae,* which the monk Dominicus Gundisalvi, assisted by the baptized Jew John Hispalensis, had translated from the Arabic. Its author was called Avicebron. The Franciscans, among them famous philosophers like Alexander of Hales and Duns Scotus, accepted its ideas and used it as a source for their own work, while the majority of the Dominicans, including Thomas Aquinas, opposed them. The importance of *Fons Vitae* as a source of medieval Neo-Platonism can hardly be exaggerated. It was not until 1840 that the great orientalist Salomon Munk discovered the real author of the book—namely, Solomon Ibn Gabirol, who, up to then, was known only as one of the greatest Spanish-Jewish poets. The Hebrew title of Ibn Gabirol's book is *Mekor Hayim* (*Fountain of Life*). It deals with the total subject matter from the point of view of the antagonism of form and matter, and establishes a hierarchy of all beings, a graduation which, on each higher level, shows a more perfect relation between form and matter. Gabirol, who continued to express his Jewish convictions in his poetry, dealt with the philosophical problems of his metaphysical work without any relation to Judaism. (W) *On the Improvement of Moral Qualities.*

Ibn Shem-Tov, Joseph

(1420-1480)

Sephardic apologist, emphasized mystical essence of Judaism. Philosopher at court of Castile, controversialist, Aristotelian; writer of *Kevod Elohim* (*Glory of God*), *En ha-Kore.*

Ibn Yahya, Gedaliah

(1515-1587)

Member of distinguished scholarly family, who wrote *Shalshelet HaKabbalah* (*Chain of Tradition*), a compound of history and fable.

Idelsohn, Abraham Zvi

(1882-1938)

Musicologist and historian of Jewish music.

Imber, Naphtali Herz

(Galicia, 1857–New York, 1909)

Poet, writer of *Hatikvah,* Jewish national anthem.

Immanuel ("God with us")

Symbolic name of messianic youth.

Immanuel (ben Solomon) of Rome

(1270-1328)

Exegete, poet, communal leader, who introduced the sonnet form and lightness of subject into Hebrew verse.

Immersion

Ceremonial bath, with special meaning for Chasidim, who also use rivers therefor.

Immortality

This became a basic belief in Talmudic days, accepted by Pharisees and rejected by Sadducees. Philosophers from Maimonides to Spinoza upheld the belief, though generally disapproving the notion that one must do good in this world in order to reap rewards in the next.

Incense

Was an essential part of sacrificial ritual; in Temple times burned at dawn and sunset; now only in Havdalah ceremony.

Inquisition

Catholic body dealing with heresy, which in 1478 became prime factor in trying accused Jewish backsliding converts. Murdered at least thirty thousand before abolition in 1834. Its chief instigator was the prior of a Dominican monastery, Tomás de Torquemada.

Intercollegiate Zionist Organization

For the Zionist education of college students.

Intermarriage

Opposed by Judaism as leading to deterioration of both faiths, since in at least one of the pair faith is sacrificed to eroticism, and not because of reason or religious doubt. Offspring will prove basically alien to one or both. Intermarriage does not improve, but confuses, human relations.

Irgun; Irgun Zvei Leumi

Organization based on Revisionist movement (Jabotinsky, Beigin).

Isaac

(Hebrew, Yitzchak, "He will laugh")

Second Patriarch; son of Abraham; father of Esau and Jacob.

Isaac ben Moses

(c. 1200-1270)

Viennese Talmudist who wrote the ritual code *Or Zarua* (*Light Diffused*).

Isaac the Blind

French cabbalist, 1200, who perfected the numerical system of that mystic movement, and added the notion of metempsychosis.

Isaiah

First of the Major (Latter) Prophets (ca. 722 B.C.E.). He preached against the evils, social and political, of his people; and against entanglement with expansionist foreign nations. His style, strong and impassioned, is marked by lyrical rhythm and impressive refrains. Like Jeremiah, legend has it that he died at the hands of assassins.

Ishmael

("Hearken, O Lord")

Son of Abraham and Hagar. Reputed ancestor of the Arab tribes.

Ishmael ben Elisha

Early tanna (Talmudic teacher) first and second centuries, who established principles of interpretation of the Law, and whose school wrote the legal commentary called Mechilta.

Ishtar

Babylonian goddess of love (Astarte). Possible connection with "Esther." See ASHTORETH.

Islam, and the Jew

In most periods Moslems have a history of oppressing Jews, as in the present era. The Turks proved the exception, having dealt with their Jews in a civilized manner. However, Moslem mistreatment of Jews does not approach the enormity of Christian persecution in Europe.

Israel

Name given Jacob after he wrestled with the angel and was disabled by his touch; the name means "wrestling with God." Name of the northern kingdom destroyed 721 B.C.E. by Assyrians. The twelve tribes, descended from Jacob's sons, are called the Children of Israel. Now the designation of the new Palestinian State.

Israel: Principal Dates

I — The Biblical Period

B.C.E.

17th to 15th centuries
The Patriarchs: Abraham, Isaac and Jacob

15th to 14th centuries
Exodus from Egypt; conquest of Canaan

13 to 11th centuries
Judges: Deborah, Gideon, Samson, etc.

mid-11th to mid-10th centuries
Saul, David, Solomon

c. 1000	David establishes capital in Jerusalem
c. 960	Solomon builds the Temple
c. 930	Division of Kingdom into Judah and Israel
721	Conquest of Kingdom of Israel by Assyrians
586	Conquest of Kingdom of Judah and destruction of Jerusalem by Babylonians

538-515	First return from Babylonian captivity. Rebuilding of Temple in Jerusalem

II – Second Temple Period

457-424	Second return. Ezra and Nehemiah
333	Alexander the Great conquers Judea
323-167	Judea under Syrian and Egyptian rule
167	Revolt of the Maccabees (Hasmoneans)
63	Pompey enters Jerusalem. Beginning of Roman domination
37	End of Hasmonean rule
37-4 C.E.	King Herod
66	Revolt of Jews against Romans
70	Destruction of Jerusalem

III – Under Foreign Rule

C.E.	
132-135	Bar Kokhba's revolt against Romans
c. 200	Completion of Mishnah (codification of Jewish Law)
352	Jewish revolt against Roman rule in Galilee
395-640	Byzantine Rule
c. 400	Completion of Jerusalem Talmud (commentary on Mishnah)
6th cent.	Justinian conquers independent Jewish island of Yotvah (Tiran) in Gulf of Akaba
614	Persian invasion, supported by Jewish army
630	Mohammed concludes treaties with Jewish settlements in southern Palestine, including Eilat

636	Beginning of Arab domination
8th, 9th cents.	Emigration of Jews from Babylon, Egypt and Syria
10th cent.	Emigration of Jews from Africa and Spain
1099	Crusaders capture Jerusalem
1141	Judah Halevi's journey to Palestine
1210	French and English rabbis settle in Palestine
1267	Jewish community in Jerusalem rebuilt by Nachmanides
1291	Mameluke conquest—end of Crusader rule
15th, 16th c.	Emigration of Jews from Spain, Portugal, Italy
1517	Ottoman conquest
c. 1530-c. 1650	Famous Jewish Cabbalists in Safed
18th cent.	Emigration of 1500 Jews from Poland, Hungary and Moravia
1799	Invasion of Napoleon
1812	Emigration of 400 Lithuanian Jews
1836	Rabbi Zevi Hirsh Kalisher advocates Jewish colonization in Land of Israel
1862	Moses Hess's "Rome and Jerusalem," advocating return to Land of Israel

IV — The Return to Zion

1870	Agricultural School founded in Mikve-Israel
1878	Petach Tikva, first agricultural settlement, founded
1882	Pinsker's "Auto-emancipation." Beginning of First Aliya. Rishon Le-Zion, Nes Ziona, Zichron Yaakov and Rosh Pina founded
1895	Theodor Herzl's "Judenstaat," advocating revival of Jewish State

1897	World Zionist Organization founded at First Zionist Congress
1904-1914	Second Aliyah—first seeds of labor movement
1909	Tel Aviv, first all-Jewish city, founded
1911	First Kvutzah (collective settlement) founded
1917	Balfour Declaration
1918	British occupation of Palestine
1920	Beginning of Third Aliyah. General Federation of Jewish Labor (Histadruth) founded
1922	British Mandate over Palestine confirmed by League of Nations
1925	Hebrew University founded on Mount Scopus
1937	Peel Commission proposes partition, with Jewish State in part of country
1939	British White Paper severely restricting Jewish immigration, land purchase and settlement
1941	Jewish State demanded in Biltmore Programme
1944	Jewish Brigade Group organized to fight in Allied Forces
1946	Anglo-American Committee recommends reversal of White Paper policy and immediate admission of 100,000 D.P's.
1947	
29 Nov.	United Nations Assembly resolves on partition of Palestine into Jewish and Arab States
Dec.	Arab attacks on Jews in towns and on roads
1948	
Jan.-Feb.	Arab "Liberation Army" attacks Jewish villages in Galilee

Feb.-Mar.	Arab attacks paralyze Jewish traffic to Jerusalem and Negev
6-10 Apr.	Haganah, Jewish defense force, opens way to Jerusalem
12 Apr.	Arab attacks in Mishmar Ha'emek repulsed
18 Apr.	Jewish counter-attack in Tiberias
22 Apr.	Jews occupy Haifa
13 May	Jaffa surrenders
14 May	Proclamation of State of Israel
15 May	End of British rule. Invasion by Arab armies
11 June	28 days' Truce imposed by United Nations
9 July	Hostilities renewed by Arabs–Lydda and Ramleh taken by Israel Defense Forces
19 July	Second Truce begins
14 Oct.	Egyptian attacks on Jewish convoy in Negev reopens hostilities there
20 Oct.	Beersheba occupied by Israel

1949

25 Jan.	Elections to First Knesset
16 Feb.	Dr. Chaim Weizmann elected President
24 Feb.	Armistice Agreement with Egypt
10 Mar.	First regular Government under David Ben-Gurion
23 Mar.	Armistice Agreement with Lebanon
3 Apr.	Armistice Agreement with Jordan
11 May	Israel joins United Nations
20 July	Armistice Agreement with Syria
Autumn	Beginning of large-scale immigration from Yemen
Spring 1950	Beginning of large-scale immigration from Iraq

1951	
30 July	Elections to Second Knesset
1 Sept.	Security Council condemns Egypt's anti-Israel blockade in Suez Canal
End 1951	Lull in large-scale immigration
1952	
9 Nov.	Death of President Weizmann
8 Dec.	Izhak Ben-Zvi elected
23 Dec.	New Government, including General Zionists
1953	
7 Dec.	Mr. Ben-Gurion resigns and retires to Sdeh Boker
1954	
26 Jan.	Mr. Moshe Sharett becomes Prime Minister
1955	
21 Feb.	Mr. Ben-Gurion returns as Minister of Defense
26 July	Elections to Third Knesset
Autumn	Czech-Egyptian arms deal
3 Nov.	New Government with Mr. Ben-Gurion as Prime Minister
1956	
29 Oct.	Sinai Operation begins and ends in four days. Destruction of Egyptian armies.
1957	
8 Mar.	Completion of Israeli withdrawal from Sinai

Israel Arab Democrats

Israeli political party which makes specific demands for the Arab community in Israel and seeks to improve the political, social and economic condition of the Asiatic and African nations.

Israeli, Isaac

(About 832-932)

Israeli, who, during the one hundred years of his life, was a famous physician and founder of an influential medical school, did not escape the fate of many other philosophers whose renown was founded upon their non-philosophical activities. But it is just that objection made by some leaders of philosophical schools that he had written his philosophical books from the medical point of view, which should attract the interest of modern scholars. For his description of the faculty of cogitation and his distinction between the impression received by "the five senses" and the post-sensory perceptions show him to have been an acute psychologist whose hints at anthropology anticipated modern discoveries. His principal work *Kitab al Istiksat,* written in Arabic, was translated into Hebrew under the title *Sefer Hayesodoth* and into Latin under the title *De Elementis.* He also wrote a treatise on definitions and commentaries on *Genesis* and the mystical *Sefer Yetzirah,* the oldest cabbalistic work which is extant. Israeli practiced medicine at Cairo, Egypt, and later at Kairwan, Tunisia. The Christian monk Constantine of Carthage translated several of Israeli's medical treatises into Latin in 1087, and used them as textbooks at the University of Salerno, the earliest university in Western Europe, but he omitted the real author's name, which was finally made known to the European public only in 1515 when *Opera Omnia Isaci* was printed at Lyons, France.

Israels, Josef

(1824-1911)

Dutch Impressionist painter,

who employed many Jewish motifs.

Isru Chag

"Binding the festival" by keeping the day after as a semi-festive period.

Issachar

Son of Jacob who founded one of the tribes of Israel.

Isserlein, Israel ben Petachiah

(1390-1460)

Austrian Talmudist, noted for his decisions on religious practices.

Isserles, Moses

(1525-1572)

Leading commentator on the standard Jewish code, Shulchan Arukh (Prepared Table).

Ivriah

Organization encouraging Hebrew education of women and children.

Ivrit

Hebrew (language).

Iyar

Eighth month of Jewish year.

Iyyun Tefillah

Prayerful devotion.

J

Jabotinsky, Vladimir

(1881-1940)

Multi-talented leader of the Revisionist Zionist movement. With Trumpeldor, founder of Jewish Legion in World War I.

Jacob

Third Patriarch, son of Isaac; later named Israel. His name may mean "grasper of the heel" (of his twin brother Esau) or "supplanter."

Jacob ben Asher

(ca. 1269-1340)

Spanish Talmudic scholar who codified Jewish law into the *Turim* (rows)—four parts.

Jacob ben Jacob Moses of Lissa

(c. 1762—Galicia, 1832)

One of the great Talmudic authorities of his day, known for his commentaries on the Schulchan Arukh and his *Derech ha-Hayyim* (*Way of Life*) (1826).

Jacob ben Meir

(1100-1171)

Known as Rabbenu Tam ("Our Perfect Master"), this grandson of Rashi was the outstanding Talmudist of his time, and chief exponent of the Tosafot (Addenda), critical comments on the Talmud. Wrote poetry, grammar notes, and responsa.

Jacob ben Moses Halevi

(1365-1427)

Also known as Jacob Molin, a leading rabbinical authority of his time, author of the often quoted *Sefer ha-Maharil* (*Religious Usages*) (first published in 1556) and many synagogal hymns.

Jacob ben Reuben

This twelfth-century Karaite lived in Constantinople and is known chiefly for his Hebrew commentaries on the Bible, called *Sefer Haosher* (*Book of Wealth*).

Jacob ben Samson

(or Simeon)
(12th century)

Pupil of Rashi and author of *Sefer ha-Elkoshi*, numerous commentaries and liturgical poems.

Jacob ben Yakar

(11th century)

A leading Talmudic authority of his time, famous as the teacher of Rashi and other noted scholars.

Jacobs, Joseph

(1854-1916)

Folklorist and historian; in his latter years professor at the Jewish Theological Seminary.

Jacob Joseph (Ha-Cohen) of Polonnoye

(d. 1782)

Author of the first book to formulate the principles and teachings of Chasidism, *Toledoth Yaakov Yosef* (*History of Jacob Joseph*), published in 1782. Although the work was publicly burned, and Rabbi Jacob Joseph driven out of several communities, his work eventually had strong influence on later Chasidic movement.

Jacobson, Israel

(1768-1828)

Protagonist of Reform Judaism in Germany.

Jagel, Abraham ben Hananiah dei Galicchi

Italian Cabbalist of sixteenth and seventeenth centuries, author of *Lekah Tov* (*Good Doc-*

trine), a type of Jewish catechism.

Jahrzeit

Annual day of memorializing death date of a loved one, marked by lighting of candles and reciting of kaddish (Yiddish).

Jahweh

Unspoken Tetragrammaton (YHVH), read Adonai (Lord). Rendering "Jehovah" is fourteenth-century. Other forms, Yah and Yahu. Found on Moabite Stele as early as ninth century B.C.E. Meaning: "I AM WHO I AM."

Jahwist

Presumed author of those portions of the Pentateuch in which God's name is Jahweh. See ELOHIST.

Javetz, Joseph ben Hayyim

Sixteenth-century Portuguese philosopher, author of *Maamar Ha-ahduth* (*Treatise on Unity*), 1554.

Javneh

Ancient town of southern Palestine, south of Jaffa, which became center of Jewish scholarship after Jerusalem was razed in 70, until its destruction in the Bar Kokhba revolt in 135.

Jebel Musa

Arabic name for Mount Sinai (Moses' Mountain).

Jedidiah

Another name of Solomon.

Jefferson, Thomas

(1743-1826)

Pre-eminent American humanist. As supporter of the First Amendment to the Constitution guaranteeing freedom of worship in the U.S., Jefferson more than any other of the Founding Fathers was responsible for establishing the tradition of religious toleration in America. To Joseph Marx of Richmond, Jefferson expressed his regret that the Jewish people, "parent and basis of all Christendom," should have in the past been singled out by the Christians "for persecution and oppression which proved that they have profited nothing from the benevolent doctrines of Him whom they profess to make the model of their principles and practice."

Jehovah

See JAHWEH.

Jehu

(841 B.C.E.–813 B.C.E.)

Founder of fifth Israelitish dynasty; killed Jezebel and all of Ahab's heirs.

Jephthah

Judge of Israel who defeated the Ammonites in battle. Promised to sacrifice the first individual who came out of his house if his campaign was successful. To his chagrin, it was his own daughter.

Jeremiah

Second of Major Prophets; preached faith in God and avoidance of political alliances, but was not heeded. Carried to Egypt after 586 B.C.E. conquest of Judah. This undaunted messenger of doom became witness to his gloomy forebodings when the first Temple was destroyed. His utterances are marked by rare poetic beauty. He died at the hands of assassins.

Jeroboam

First king of Israel, who brought about schism in united kingdom, 933 B.C.E.

Jerusalem

(City of Peace)

Capital of the Israelite nation, symbol of Judaism and monotheism for both Eastern and Western worlds.

Jerusalem Post

Leading English language daily in Israel.

Jeshurun

Israel.

Jeshua ben Judah

(Abu Al-Faraj Ibn Asad)

Eleventh-century Karaite scholar who translated the Pentateuch into Arabic and reformed the Karaite law concerning consanguine marriage.

Jesus

Greek form of Joshua. Early followers called him Messiah (Christos). Put to death legendarily by Roman tribunal for calling himself King of the Jews; nothing in Jewish rights or jurisprudence could have permitted the trial described in New Testament. Only small group were Christians at time of Titus' destruction of Jerusalem (70 C.E.). Many men were proclaimed Messiahs in those troubled days, and Jews were generally tolerant of sectarians. Jesus seems to have taught the ways of the Essenes, a sect of moralizing ascetics, without practical striving or attitudes. Employing the case of the fabled William Tell, Georg Brandes wrote a book called *Jesus: A Myth.*

Jethro

Father-in-law and adviser of Moses.

Jew

Derived from name Judah.

Jew Bishop

Official designation in medieval Germany for head of Jewish community.

Jew Hat

A pointed head covering Jews were forced to wear in parts of medieval Central Europe, notably Germany.

Jew Porcelain

In 1769 Prussian Jews were compelled by King Frederick to purchase porcelain, at a time when sales of this product were poor. One of the forced purchasers was Moses Mendelssohn.

Jew School

Luther's derogatory name for synagogue.

Jew Spot

A piece of cloth, generally yellow, worn by Jews on their coats in parts of medieval Central

Europe, especially Germany, as ordered by the authorities. This humiliating statute remained in force in Germany to the eighteenth century. Revived by Hitler two centuries later.

Jew Suess (Joseph Oppenheimer)

(1692-1738)

Financial adviser of the Duke of Württemberg, executed after Duke Alexander's death.

Jew Tax

Inaugurated by Vespasian after destruction of Temple. Also, special fee collected until the middle of the nineteenth century from Jewish travelers crossing borders within Prussia and Russia.

Jewish Agency

Organization of Zionists and non-Zionists to consolidate State of Israel, further ingathering of the exiles, and fostering Jewish unity; established under League of Nations Mandate, 1922.

Jewish Agricultural Society

American organization encouraging return of Jews to the soil.

Jewish Board of Guardians

New York group concerned with problems of the child and the family.

Jewish Family Service

New York organization concerned with family difficulties, including those arising from ex-inmates of prisons.

Jewish Institute of Religion

Liberal seminary founded by Stephen S. Wise in 1922, New York; now combined with HEBREW UNION COLLEGE.

Jewish Legion

Jewish voluntary fighting force organized during first World War by Vladimir Jabotinsky and Joseph Trumpeldor.

Jewish National Fund (Keren Kayemet LeYisrael)

Founded 1901 to gather funds

and acquire land in Palestine (Israel).

Jewish Publication Society of America

Founded 1888 in Philadelphia, to publish and reprint worthwhile works of Jewish literature.

Jewish Sabbath Alliance

American group seeking strict Sabbath observance among employers and employees, and carrying on agitation against proposed new, floating Sabbath, calendar.

Jewish Science

A Jewish religious movement founded by Rabbi Morris Lichtenstein in New York, 1922, to counteract the influence of Christian Science upon Jews. After his death in 1938 the rabbi's widow took over leadership of the tiny group.

Jewish Theological Seminary of America

Conservative seminary organized in New York 1886 by Sabato Morais and associates; reorganized 1902, with Solomon Schechter as president.

Jews' College

London theological seminary founded in 1856.

Jezebel

Pagan princess of Tyre, spouse of King Ahab, enemy of prophet Elijah.

Joab

Commander-in-chief of David's army.

Job

The most profound Biblical dramatic poem, centering around an ancient chieftain, who, after great suffering, endeavored—against three foil characters—to interpret the purposefulness of Divine Providence. Its authorship was traditionally ascribed to Moses, but higher criticism assigns it a postexilic date.

Jochanan bar Napacha

(c. 199-279)

Founded his own academy in

Tiberias. Considered the chief amora of Palestine in his day.

Jochanan ben Zaccai

Most eminent TANNA of first century; head of the PHARISEES; advocated peace with Romans, who permitted him, after the siege of Jerusalem, to open new academy at Javneh. After the destruction of the Temple he escaped the beleaguered city by being carried out in a coffin. As the Rabban he held together a disheartened people in Israel.

Joel

One of the twelve Minor PROPHETS; time of activity indefinite.

Jonah

Reluctant prophet against Nineveh. Book contains legend of the whale.

Jonathan ben Uzziel

First century TANNA, said to have written Aramaic (TARGUM) translation of the Prophets.

Jordan

Chief river of Israel; symbol of ZION.

José ben José

(Called Hayathom, the orphan)

One of the earliest composers of piyyutim, presumed to have lived in Palestine in the seventh century.

Joseph (the fertile)

Son of Jacob who became premier of Egypt. Father of two tribes—Manasseh and Ephraim.

Joseph ben Jacob ibn Zaddik

(Abu Omar)

Twelfth-century Spanish rabbi, poet and philosopher, author of *Sefer Haolam Ha-Katon* (*Microcosm*), a philosophy of religion based on the Neo-Platonism of his day, but influenced by Aristotle.

Joseph ben Nathan Hamekanne

(called the Zealot)

Thirteenth-century exegete,

author of *Teshuvoth Ha-Minim* (*Replies to Heretics*), discussions between him and other French rabbis with Christian clerics.

Joseph ben Samuel Tov-Elem

Eleventh-century Talmudist of France. Writer of piyyutim. His decisions often quoted by Rashi.

Joseph ha-Cohen

Sixteenth-century Italian historian; author of *Emek ha-Bakhah* (*Valley of Tears*), recounting persecutions of Jews, tenth to sixteenth centuries.

Josephus, Flavius

(ca. 37-106)

Famed historian of Judaism who, when defending Jerusalem against Rome, capitulated before the siege in an effort to save his people. After the destruction he departed for Rome, where he remained as an apologete for Judaism. His appeal: "Let us not blaspheme the gods of other people." His classics, *Antiquities of the Jews* and *The Wars of the Jews*, are main sources of post-Biblical historical knowledge.

Joshua ("God help")

Military successor to Moses; conqueror of Canaan.

Joshua ben Hananiah

(c. 35—c. 125)

Palestinian tanna, disciple of Johanan ben Zakkai, who succeeded his master as head of the Great Sanhedrin in Javneh. He opposed rebellion against Rome and rejected the asceticism to which many of his colleagues turned after the destruction of the Temple.

Joshua ben Levi

Talmudist in Lydda, third century. As hero of legendry, robs angel of sword, reaches Paradise alive, like Job defends Divine Providence.

Josiah

(639 B.C.E.-608 B.C.E.)

During his reign over Judah, a basic part of the book of Deuteronomy was found in the Temple, and with this book as his guide, he began a program of reform, consisting, in part, of cleansing the Temple of idolatrous objects and rites.

Jubilee

(Heb. "yovel"—shofar blast)

Period each fifty years when original distribution of land was re-established, and Jewish slaves were liberated.

Judaeo-Persian

A hybrid language written in Hebrew characters and containing in addition to the Hebrew splinters as well as combinations from the Aramaic, Arabic, Turkish, Russian and archaic Persian. Used by the Jews of Iran, and employed in an extensive literature.

Judah

Fourth son of Jacob, ancestor of tribe of Judah. Likened to a lion's whelp.

Judah

Name of southern Kingdom; came under the hegemony of Babylon; rebelled against Nebuchadnezzar who then brought his army in force and destroyed Jerusalem and the Temple in 586 B.C.E.

Judah ben Ezekiel

Talmudist who founded school at Pumbedita, Babylonia. (Third cent.)

Judah ben Samuel of Regensburg

(d. 1217)

Known as "He-Chassid"—"the Saint"—father of Jewish mysticism in Germany, 13th and 14th centuries. Chief work, *Sefer Chasidim* (*Book of the Pious*).

Judah ha-Nasi

(135-220)

Great-grandson of Gamaliel I, known as Prince (patriarch) of the Palestinian community. Cited in the Talmud simply as "Rabbi," he committed the Oral Law —Mishnah—to writing.

Judah Loew ben Bezaleel

(Poznań, 1520–Prague, 1609)

Famed ethical and homiletic writer, who as Rabbi of Prague is central figure of Golem legend. Contributed to Talmudic and cabbalistic literature, and highly regarded by his contemporaries.

Judaism

The generic term applying not alone to the religion of Israel but to most evidences of Jewish history and culture. It is the unifying force that creates fraternal feeling among most of the world's Jews.

Judaizers

Persons who, though regarded as Christians, secretly observed Jewish rites. The early Catholic Church vehemently opposed vestiges of Judaizing among its adherents. During the century preceding the expulsion from Spain (1492), many Jews were driven to outwardly profess Christianity. Many Judaizers eventually emigrated in order to practice their religion openly; others gradually lost touch with their traditions and practices. In our time Judaizing is carried on in the Soviet Union and its satellites on a large scale, as all Jewish traditional feelings and other ceremonial activities are curtailed.

Judas Maccabeus (Hammerer)

Hero of the Hasmonean revolt against the Greek-Syrians (167 B.C.E.). Rededicated and sanctified the Temple, desecrated by pagan rites. Commemorated through Chanukah festival. Judas fell in battle, 161.

Juderia

Jewish quarter; Sephardic.

Judges

Bible book relating frequent decline and restoration of Israel's national life, with sometimes anarchy and paganism; and the national heroes that brought about deliverance.

Judith of Bethulia

This widow enticed and assassinated Holofernes, commander of the troops that had laid siege to her town.

Justice

Social consciousness, the duty of the individual to society, his personal responsibility for a just social order, is a basic concept of Judaism. A pious Jew cannot, according to Jewish teaching, isolate himself in individual piety and be considered a good Jew. He is asked to remember that he is part of a world which is ruled by a God "who loves justice and hates iniquity" (Ps. 4:2). The attitude of Judaism toward social justice is illustrated by the fact that a great and holy man is called a "tzaddik" ("man of justice") rather than a "saint"—a term unknown in Jewish theology.

Justinian

Emperor of East Roman realm (527-565), erroneously called "the Just." Originator of savage anti-Jewish legislation.

K

Kabak, Aaron Abraham

(Lithuania, 1880 – Jerusalem, 1944)

Prolific Hebrew novelist and short story writer.

Kabbalat Shabbat

"Receiving the Sabbath" by recitation of psalms and hymns immediately before regular evening service.

Kaddish

From the Aramaic for "holy." Doxology following study period, now recited also at death of parents and other relatives by sons. Recited at daily services for eleven months if for father or mother, and also on anniversary of death. Used in all public worship as glorification of the Holy Name.

Kadmonim

See POSEKIM.

Kafka, Franz

(German, 1883-1924)

Austrian-born novelist, whose influence became international 20 years after death. A lonely, tormented figure, who suffered from tuberculosis. Published only few stories during lifetime. Three posthumous novels—*The Castle, The Trial, Amerika*—notable for atmosphere of paranoia, the individual struggling against anonymous powers. Fantastic motives combined with detailed realism. (W) *The Great Wall of China, The Metamorphosis.*

Kaftan

Long black medieval coat worn in traditional Jewish circles of Eastern Europe up to our time.

Kahal

1. Title of a book by the Jewish renegade Jacob Brofman in Russia (1869), containing charges similar to those in the *Protocols of Zion,* another framed anti-Jewish plot deriving from a Russian publication.

2. Jewish communal self-government, Middle Ages and early modern period. Justice was administered through Bet Din (religio-civil court).

Kalir, Eleazar

(fl. ca. 750?)

Palestine liturgical poet.

Kalisher, Zevi Hirsch

(Lissa, 1795–Thorn, 1874)

Rabbi who labored in early Zionist movement, writing *Derishat Tziyon (Yearning for Zion)*; advocated colonization societies, agricultural schools; spiritual father of Mizrachi (religious Zionist) movement.

Kallah

Bride.

Kallen, Horace Meyer

(1882––)

Of all philosophical branches, it is aesthetics that attracts Kallen's highest enduring interest. But he holds that active participation in political and economic movements is of greater importance and more urgent. Kallen has taken a leading part in the defense of civil rights, of freedom of thought and conscience, in advocating the demands of American labor, in the foundation of consumers' co-operatives, and in Jewish affairs, not least in Zionism. (W) *The*

Liberal Spirit, The Education of Free Men.

Kaplan, Mordecai M.

Lithuanian-born rabbi (1881); founder of the American Reconstructionist movement; professor at Jewish Theological Seminary; author of *Judaism as a Civilization* and other works.

Kapote

Traditional long black coat worn by Eastern European Jews.

Kapparah

(Atonement Sacrifice)

Traditional "scapegoat" sacrificed the day before Yom Kippur. A rooster or hen, according to sex of person, is swung three times around head of person, with appropriate prayer. The slain animal symbolically takes on the suppliant's guilt.

Karaites

(Bene Mikra, Sons of the Book)

Jewish sect of Middle East, beginning eighth century, which accepts the Bible law but rejects the Talmud.

Karet

"Being cut off" from the people; Biblical punishment which might become capital or consist of early natural death.

Kashah

Query.

Kashern

Verb signifying process of rendering foods and utensils kosher under ritual laws applying to the cuisine and to Passover.

Katz

Jewish family name formed from initials of *kohen tzedek,* priest of righteousness.

Kavvanah

Direction of heart toward God and prayer; mystical overtones among cabbalists.

Kedushah

(Holiness)

When the reader or cantor

repeats the Amidah (standing prayer), the congregation rises for this antiphonal chant of a doxology from Bible verses proclaiming oneness and sanctity of the Lord.

Kehillah

See KAHAL, 2.

Kellner, Leon

(Tarnow, 1859–Vienna, 1928)

Philologist; English scholar; editor of Herzl's papers.

Keren ha-Yesod

Foundation Fund, to carry on activities of the World Zionist Organization and the Jewish Agency (Zionist and non-Zionist) in developing Palestine (Israel); founded 1920.

Keriah

Rending outer garment as sign of grief; ordained by Bible to prevent excesses of mourning in ancient days.

Keriat ha-Torah

Reading of the Pentateuch—portion applying to the occasion.

Kest

Meals (Yiddish) given to newly wed couple by bride's parents, sometimes for years, in Eastern Europe.

Kether Torah

Crown of the Torah—generally of silver, with tinkling bells placed over upper ends of the wooden poles (etz chaim) on which the holy scroll is wound.

Ketubah

(Writing)

Traditional marriage contract, detailing duties of wife and husband, and providing money penalties for divorcement of wife.

Ketuvim

Third part of Bible—holy writings—from Psalms to Chronicles. See HAGIOGRAPHA.

Kfar

Village, settlement.

Kibbud av va-em

Honor to father and mother.

Kibbutz

Communal agricultural settlement in Israel.

Kiddush

(Sanctification)

Blessing over wine before and during Sabbaths and festivals. Recited in synagogue, for travelers who at one time lodged there, at end of evening service—except on Passover eves, when recitation is reserved for the seder services.

Kiddush Ha-Shem

Sanctification of the Divine Name—through sacrifice and martyrdom and also through high order of ethical living.

Kilayim

(Two Kinds)

Biblically prohibited hybridization of plants or animals.

Kimchi, David ben Joseph

(1160-1235)

French Jewish commentator and grammarian, one of whose important works is *Michlol* (*Perfection*), a dictionary of Biblical Hebrew. (W) *Book of the Covenant.*

Kimchi, Joseph ben Isaac

(ca. 1105-1170)

Spanish-French grammarian, translator, and polemicist.

Kinah

(Lamentation)

Elegy in poetic (piyyut) structure recited on Jewish days of mourning.

King of Jerusalem

Until twentieth century, one title of the Austrian Kaiser.

Kings (Melakhim)

Two Bible books covering royal period in Israel and Judah

(there were two kingdoms after Solomon), from Solomon to the release of Jehoiachim from imprisonment in Babylonia. Probably written 600 B.C.E.

Kiryat Sefer

Bibliographical Judaica periodical published in Jerusalem, beginning in 1924.

Kishinef

Scene of Russian pogroms, April, 1903 and October, 1905.

Kislev

Third month of Jewish year.

Kiss, Joseph

(Hungarian, 1843-1921)

Most genuine Hungarian poet. Taught in Hebrew schools. Best-known ballads: *Simon Judith, The Lady of Gedovar, Against the Stream*—the latter being sung, at one time, in Russian synagogues.

Kittel

White robe worn on high holidays and other occasions, symbolizing remembrance of death, purity, or both.

Klal Yisrael

Phrase meaning the entirety of Israel.

Klatzkin, Jakob

(Poland, 1882–New York, 1948)

Hebrew nationalist, translator, encyclopedist.

Klaus

Small East European house of prayer.

Klausner, Joseph

(b. Russia, 1874)

Editor; professor at Odessa; after 1925 professor of modern Hebrew literature at Hebrew University; wrote life of Jesus from Jewish viewpoint. (W) *History of the New Hebrew Literature, Millon shel Kiss, History of Messianology, Jesus the Nazarite.*

Kneeling

Common during worship in Biblical times; now forbidden except on Rosh ha-Shanah and Yom Kippur.

Knesset

Assembly; Israel's parliament.

Kodesh Kadashim

Holy of Holies. Inner sanctum of Tabernacle, entered only on Yom Kippur by high priest.

Koheleth

See ECCLESIASTES.

Kohen, Cohen

Priest; Aaronite.

Kohler, Kaufmann

(1843-1926)

German-born Reform rabbi, who served as president of the Hebrew Union College and wrote important theological works. (W) *Jewish Theology, Guide for Instruction in Judaism, Studies in Jewish Literature, Heaven and Hell, The Origins of the Synagog and Church, Personal Reminiscences.*

Kohut, Alexander

(Hungary, 1842–New York, 1894)

Rabbi, Talmudist, author of *Aruch Completum,* Talmud dictionary. (W) *Ethics of the Fathers.*

Kohut, Rebekah

(1864-1951)

Social worker; second wife of Alexander Kohut, stepmother of Jewish educator and scholar, George Alexander Kohut. (W) *My Portion, As I Know Them.*

Kol-Bo

("All is therein")

Anthology of laws concerning all the days of the year, services, dietary, and other rituals, based on Shulchan Arukh. Also a prayer book containing all prayers of the year, and various other interpretive writings and responsa.

Kol Nidre

(All Vows)

Public declaration of uncertain origin, chanted thrice at beginning of Yom Kippur services, canceling all forced or harmful personal vows.

Kook, Abraham Isaac

(Courland, 1865–Jerusalem, 1935)

Distinguished Talmudist and cabbalist who served as chief rabbi of Palestine.

Korach

Joined with the brothers Dathan and Abiram; rebelled against Moses.

Korban

Offering; sacrifice.

Kos shel Eliyahu

The special cup of wine set aside for Elijah, the perennial visitor, at the seder.

Kosher

This word means ritually proper, and in the main is applied to food prepared in accord with traditional Jewish law.

Krauskopf, Joseph

(Germany, 1858–Philadelphia, 1923)

Popular exponent of Liberal Judaism.

Krauss, Samuel

(1866-1948)

Voluminous writer on philology of Jewish lore.

Krochmal, Nachman

(1785-1840)

Galician scholar who attempted reconciliation of Judaism with modern thought in his *Moreh Nebuche ha-Zeman* (*Guide to the Perplexed of Our Time*).

Kuppah

(Basket)

Container or organization for collection of alms. Cf. Kuppat Cholim—box for the ill; agency for healing.

Kuzari

Work by Judah Halevi, telling of conversion of Russian Khazars to Judaism, after a rabbi proves to a doubting king the supremacy of the Jewish faith.

Kvittel

(Yiddish)

A supplicatory note addressed to a tzaddik, living or dead.

Kvutzah

(Group)

Workers or farmers village, in which they own all property in common. First such group established 1899 in Palestine.

(*Zionist Archives and Library of the Palestine Foundation Fund*)

PLATE 49. Nahum Sokolov

(*Zionist Archives and Library of the Palestine Foundation Fund*)

PLATE 50. Arthur James Balfour

(*Zionist Archives and Library of the Palestine Foundation Fund*)

PLATE 51. Dr. Theodor Herzl

(*Courtesy of Zionist Archives and Library*)

PLATE 52. Martin Buber

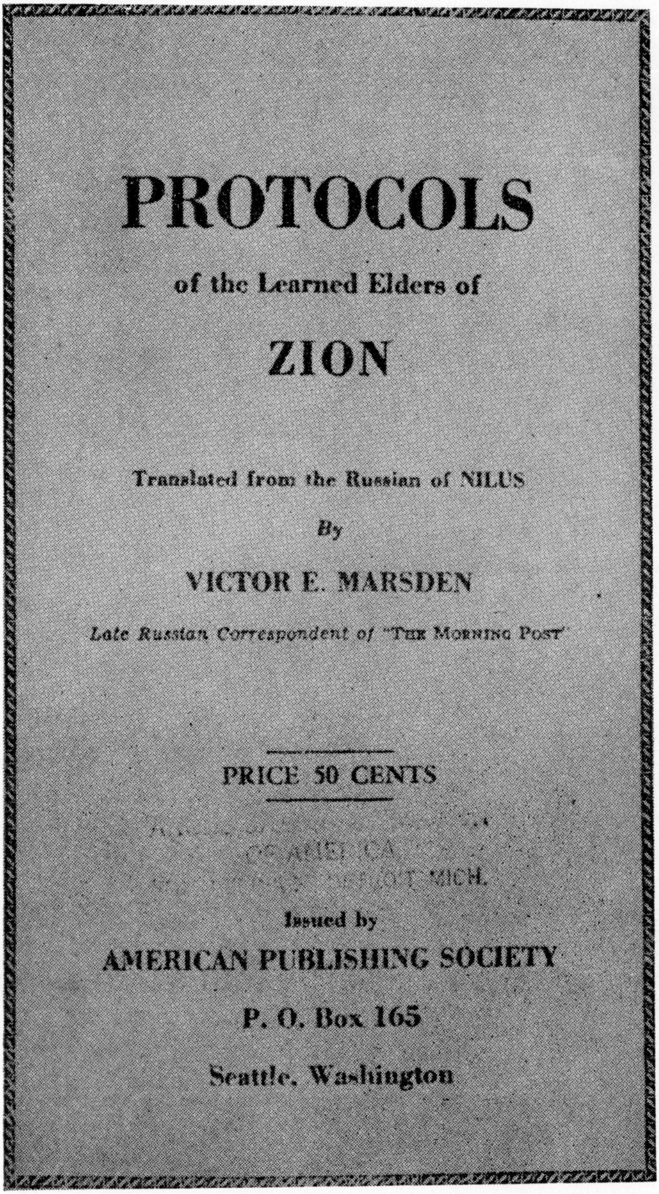

PROTOCOLS

of the Learned Elders of

ZION

Translated from the Russian of NILUS

By

VICTOR E. MARSDEN

Late Russian Correspondent of "THE MORNING POST"

PRICE 50 CENTS

Issued by

AMERICAN PUBLISHING SOCIETY

P. O. Box 165

Seattle, Washington

PLATE 53. Circulating Anti-Semitic Propaganda, the Forged *Protocols* (19th Century)

(From a drawing by S. Begg)

PLATE 54. The Third Trial of Captain Dreyfus: The Prisoner before the Court Martial at Rennes

(*From* The Scourge of the Swastika)

PLATE 55. Warsaw Round-up

Foreign Office,

November 2nd, 1917.

Dear Lord Rothschild,

I have much pleasure in conveying to you, on behalf of His Majesty's Government, the following declaration of sympathy with Jewish Zionist aspirations which has been submitted to, and approved by, the Cabinet.

"His Majesty's Government view with favour the establishment in Palestine of a national home for the Jewish people, and will use their best endeavours to facilitate the achievement of this object, it being clearly understood that nothing shall be done which may prejudice the civil and religious rights of existing non-Jewish communities in Palestine, or the rights and political status enjoyed by Jews in any other country"

I should be grateful if you would bring this declaration to the knowledge of the Zionist Federation.

PLATE 56. The Balfour Declaration

(*Courtesy of Jewish Theological Seminary of America*)

PLATE 57. Torah Ark
from Cairo, Egypt, 13th Century

(*Courtesy of Jewish Theological Society of America*)

PLATE 58. Torah Crown. Silver. Partly Gilt, Lemberg (Lwow), 1774

PLATE 59. Spice Container (Besamim Box)
Silver, Frankfort-on-the-Main, 1550 Inscription date, 1651

PLATE 60.

Top: The Cantor chanting prayers in front of the open Ark, holding one of the Scrolls, which is adorned with silver bells and breast plate.

Bottom: Reading from the Torah, indicating the words with a silver pointer shaped in the form of a human hand (the Yad).

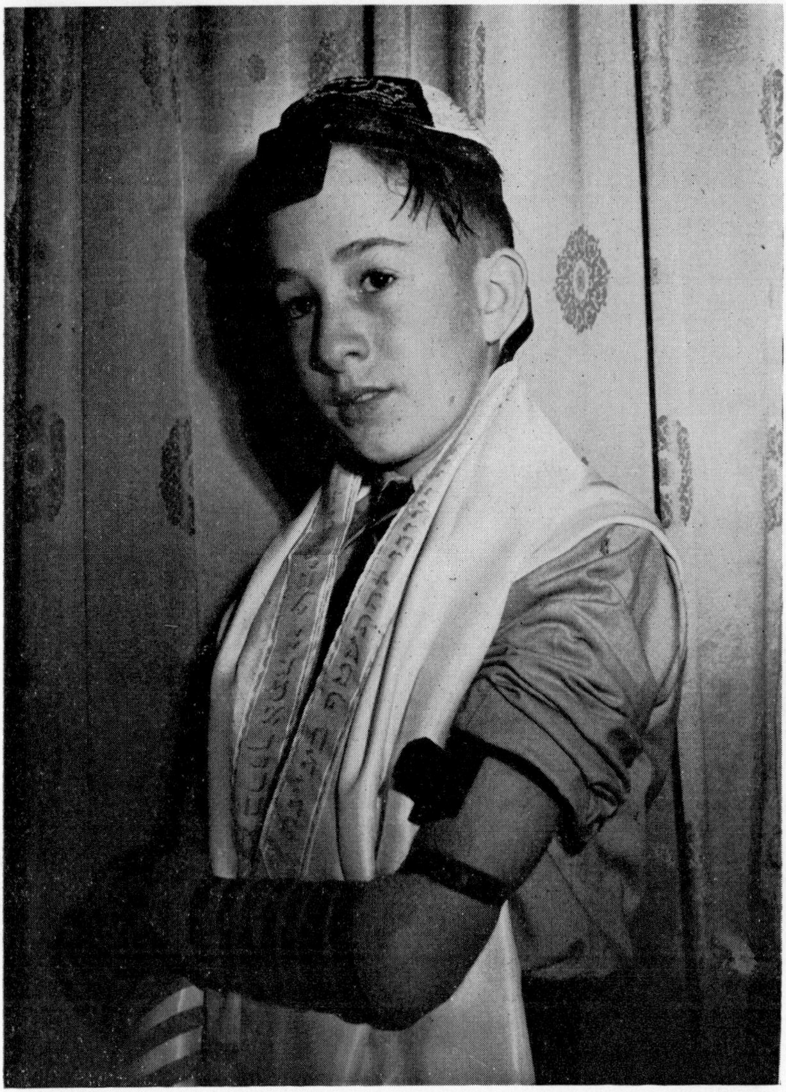

PLATE 61. Boy Saying Morning Prayers with Phylacteries

PLATE 62. The Blessing of the Candles on Friday Night

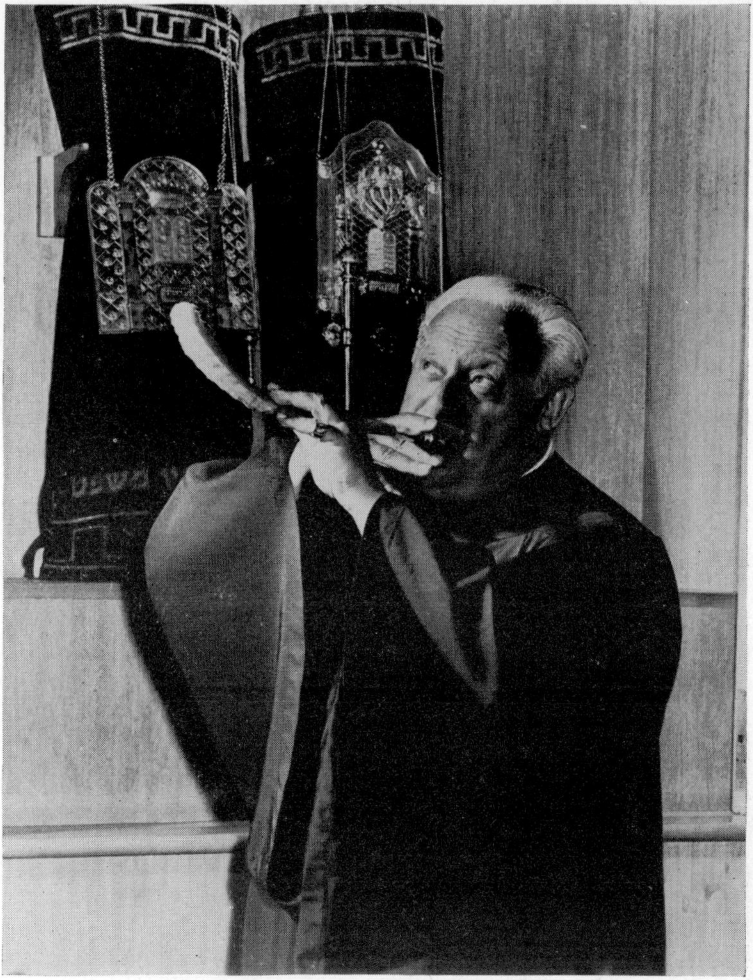

PLATE 63. Blowing the Shofar

On Rosh Hashonnah, the New Year Day, the Shofar, or Ram's Horn, is sounded in the Synagogue as a call to conscience. The Shofar is also sounded at the close of the Day of Atonement Services

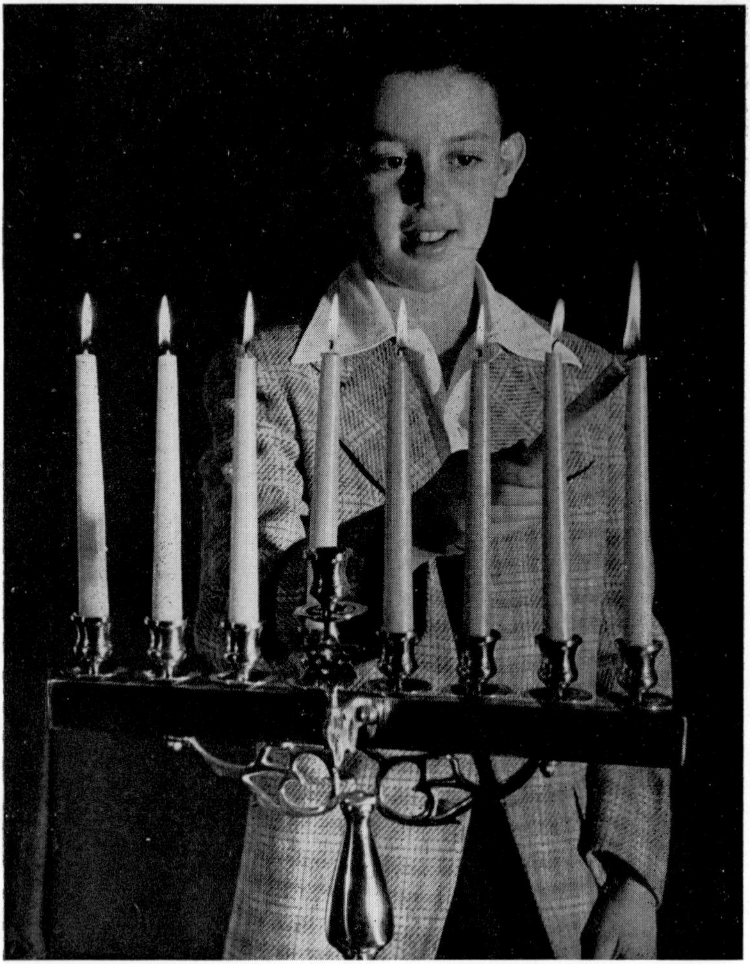

PLATE 64. Lighting the Channukah Candles

On Channukah, the Feast of Dedication, candles are lighted, beginning with one on the first night and increasing to eight on the last night of the Festival

L

Labor Zionism

Poale Zion, a socialist group, favors remaking Israel on Marxist basis; the Mapai party stems from this organization.

Lachower, Fishel

(b. 1883, Poland)

Hebrew book and magazine editor; author of *History of Modern Hebrew Literature.*

Ladino

(Latin)

Dialect of Sephardic Jews, based on medieval Spanish vocabulary, with Hebrew additions. Unlike the Yiddish dialect of Ashkenazic Jews, it has contributed very little to modern literature.

Lag ba-Omer

(33rd Day of Omer)

Semi-holiday of unknown origin. Celebrated as Arbor Day in Israel; a children's festival, with picnics and archery games. Thought to commemorate Bar Kokhba's uprising.

Lamdan

Talmudic scholar.

Lamed-Vav Tzaddikim

The 36 righteous men in every generation, not known, who, according to the Talmud, justify the continued existence of humanity.

Lamentations

Grieving chapters over sinful people and destruction of Jerusalem, ascribed to Jeremiah. Read on Tishah B'Av.

Lamerchav

Organ of the Achduth Avodah party in Israel.

Lampronti, Isaac

(1679-1756, Ferrara)

Author of encyclopedia of rabbinic learning, *Pachad Yitzchak* (*Reverence of Isaac*).

Landau, Ezekiel ben Judah

(1713-1793)

Rabbi of Prague; great Talmudist of his day; his responsa, *Noda bi-Yehudah*, are still authoritative.

Latif, Isaac

(Toledo, 1220–Jerusalem, 1290)

Mystic who wrote *Shaar ha-Shamayim* (*Gate to Heaven*).

Lazarus, Emma

(1849-1887)

American poet and translator, one of whose sonnets is inscribed on the Statue of Liberty. (W) *Songs of a Semite, The Dance of Death, By the Waters of Babylon.*

Lazarus, Moritz

(1824-1903)

German liberal philosopher and psychologist; author of *Psychology of Nations* and *Ethik des Judentums.* (W) *Das Leben der Seele, Treu und Frei, Der Prophet Jeremias.*

Lebensohn, Abraham Dov

(1789-1878)

Hebrew poet, and leader of Haskalah in Lithuania.

Lechah Dodi

An acrostic song to welcome the Sabbath Bride; composed, sixteenth century, by Solomon ha-Levi Alkabez.

Lechem ha-Panim

"Bread of His Countenance";

12 loaves of shewbread on the Sanctuary table, replaced each Sabbath, symbolic of the 12 tribes.

Lehachis

Out of spite.

Lehavdil

To distinguish sharply.

Leivick, Halpern

(1888—)

This leading Yiddish poet and dramatist came from Russia to continue his writing in America.

Lekavod

Honoring.

Lemach Scroll

Apocryphal work referred to in several ancient texts; copy found among the Dead Sea Scrolls. The Book of Lemach is a commentary on Genesis, in Hebrew and Aramaic.

Leo Hebraeus

See ABRAVANEL, JUDAH.

Leshanah Tovah tikatev (u)

"May you be inscribed for a good year"—customary New Year's greeting.

Leshon ha-Kodesh

Holy Tongue; Hebrew.

Leshon Sagi Nehor

"Expression of great delight" —the custom of employing such contrary euphemisms as calling the blind "men of much light" and the cemetery "House of Life."

Lessing, Gotthold Ephraim

(Germany, 1729-1781)

German critic and dramatist. One of the very distinguished Continental liberals. Gave up clerical career to become playwright. With Moses Mendelssohn and Nicolai, produced critical journal. *Laokoon,* famous treatise defining differences between poetry and other arts. *Nathan the Wise,* important drama pleading religious tolerance, has as central character a figure based on his friend Mendelssohn. Also author of a play, *Die Juden.*

Levayah

Funeral.

Levi ben Abraham ben Chayim

(1245-1316)

French Talmudist, philosopher, and master of all knowledge; wrote encyclopedia *Sefer ha-Kolel.*

Levi ben Gershon

See GERSONIDES.

Leviathan

Sea monster mentioned in Job, of which the pious will eat at the resurrection.

Levinsohn, Isaac Ber

(1788-1860, Russia)

Pioneer of the Haskalah (Enlightenment) movement seeking closer ties between Jew and non-Jew through some attenuation of Judaism. (W) *Te'uddah be-Yisrael, Bet Yehudah, Efes Dammin.*

Levita, Elijah

(Germany, 1468–Venice, 1549)

Hebrew grammarian and lexicographer. (W) *Sefer ha-Bahur, Sefer ha-Zikronot.*

Levites

Members of the tribe of Levi, serving as Temple attendants under the priests (kohanim).

Leviticus

Third Book of Moses; also Book of Atonement and Holiness. Sacrifices, ritual, priestly and health laws, general precepts.

Levy, Asser van Swellem

(d. 1680)

One of first Jewish settlers in New Amsterdam. He won equal rights for his brethren from Governor Peter Stuyvesant.

Levy, Uriah Phillips

(1792-1862)

Distinguished American naval officer, who suffered from anti-Semitism but became first Jewish commodore.

Lévy-Bruhl, Lucien

(1857-1939)

When Lévy-Bruhl died, the Sorbonne, the University of Paris, deplored the loss of one of the most brilliant teachers; the French people mourned a staunch defender of human rights and a convinced and active republican and democrat; tens of thousands of political refugees, of human beings persecuted for religious or racial reasons, felt themselves deprived of the moral and material support of a true humanitarian; and experts in sociology, psychology, philosophy, epistemology and many branches of linguistics began to miss the inspiring influence of a scholar whose ideas had offered them new aspects. Lévy-Bruhl had published solid and significant works on the history of German and French philosophy before he began his important investigations of primitive society. He penetrated into the soul of prelogical man who thought mystically. The philosophical problem that was raised by the results of his inquiries can be formulated as follows: Although all physio-psychological processes of perception of the primitive man are the same as those of modern, logical man—although both have the same structure of brain, the primitive man does not perceive as modern man does. The external world which the primitive man perceives is different from that of modern man, just as the social environments of both are different. Death forced Lévy-Bruhl to commit to his successors the responsibility of drawing further conclusions from his statements. (W) *History of Modern Philosophy in France.*

Lex talionis

(Law of Retaliation)

The Biblical law of "an eye for an eye, a tooth for a tooth," (Ex. 21) never interpreted literally but as applying to appropriate payment in money, to prevent undue demands for punishment.

Lifnim mishurat haddin

Beyond and above legalism.

Lilien, Ephraim Moses

(Galicia, 1874–Germany, 1925)

Line artist, book ornamenter, with Jewish motifs.

Lilienblum, Moses Leib

(Russia, 1843-1910)

Maskil (member of Haskalah movement) who criticized Talmudic education, but became a pioneer in seeking Palestinian colonization. (W) *Hatat Neurim, Olam ha-Tohu, Derek La'abor Golim, Derek Teshuba, Zerubabel.*

Lilienthal, Max

(1815-1882)

German-born leader of American Reform movement.

Lilith

(Nocturne)

Primordial female demon.

Lipsky, Louis

(1876—–)

American Zionist, publicist, editor and writer.

Little Yom Kippur

(Y. K. Katan)

Eve of Rosh Chodesh and other occasions when some Jews fast, with part of Yom Kippur ritual.

Loew, Judah ben Bezalel

See JUDAH LOEW.

Lost Tribes

The ten tribes who constituted the kingdom of Israel and who mysteriously disappeared without trace after the conquest of Shalmaneser of Assyria. Many have traced them to various parts of the world, but they seem actually to have been assimilated with their Assyrian captors and surrounding nations.

Lots, Feast of

See PURIM.

Love thy neighbor

Cardinal precept of Judaism. Proclaimed and stressed in the Old Testament.

Lulav

Palm frond, one of four species waved at Sukkoth services (others are citron, myrtle, willow). These plants are interpreted as representing various types of man.

Lunel

Southern France; center of Talmudic study, eleventh to thirteenth centuries.

Luria, Isaak ben Solomon Ashkenazi

(1534-1572)

Jerusalem-born mystic, educated in Egypt, died in Safed. Lived as hermit, and proclaimed encounters with prophets in his sleep. Followers considered him Messiah ben Joseph, forerunner of Messiah ben David. Known through works of his disciple, Chaim Vital.

Luzzatto, Moses Chaim

(1707-1747)

Some occurrences in Luzzatto's life show a parallel to that of Spinoza. Like Spinoza, he was excommunicated from his co-religionists. Luzzatto remained a faithful Jew, ardently devoted to the cause of Judaism. He even felt himself, like the Messiah, bound to rescue the Jewish people from danger and misery, and he believed that the study of the Cabbala would enable him to perform that mission. Notwithstanding pressure on the part of orthodox rabbis, Luzzatto did not turn his thoughts from the mysticism that not only incited his loftiest aspirations but also inspired him to the conception of high ethical principles. Luzzatto was a versatile and gifted writer whose Hebrew style is much admired. He composed a drama, many liturgical poems and philosophical treatises in Hebrew, while his mystical works were written in Aramaic. His best-known book is *Mesillat Yesharim* (*Path of the Upright,* 1740) which has been compared with Bunyan's *Pilgrim's Progress* though it was not influenced by the latter. In 1746, Luzzatto emigrated to the Holy Land where he died shortly after his arrival. (W) *Layesharim Tehillah* (*Praise to the Upright*).

M

Maamad

"Station"—groups of lay people who assisted the Levites at the daily sacrifices one week a year.

Maariv

Evening prayer. In case of delay, it may be recited any time before dawn.

Maaser

Tithe; the tenth part of income prescribed for charitable purposes by the Torah.

Maavarot

Immigrant transition camps in Israel.

Machpelah

(Doubled)

Burial cave of Patriarchs near Hebron.

Machzor

(Repetition)

Prayer book for festivals. Best known medieval machzor by Simchah ben Samuel of Vitri.

Madagascar

Island home of Semitic-looking tribe who observe circumcision and Sabbath.

Magen David

"Shield of David"—hexagram

of crossed triangles, first found in Sidon, seventh century B.C.E., on a seal. It received its present name and acceptance as major Jewish symbol, 1148.

Maggid

Preacher; generally itinerant, and popular because of his clever parables.

Magnes, Judah Leon

(1877-1948)

American Reform rabbi who was a Zionist leader and became first president of the Hebrew University, 1925. In his latter years he naïvely advocated Arab-Jewish alliance.

Mah Nishtanah

"Wherefor is different?": First words of the Four Questions asked by the youngest reader at the seder table.

Mahamad

Governing body of trustees in a Sephardic synagogue.

Maimon, Salomon

(1753-1800)

Immanuel Kant recognized Maimon as the most acute of all his critics. The famous author of the *Critique of Pure Reason* probably knew what hardships Maimon had endured before he could publish his *Versuch ueber die Transzendentalphilosophie,* in which he successfully dealt with problems not understandable to the great majority of German thinkers of that time. When Maimon, in 1778, left his native village of Nieszwicz, Lithuania, he had been trained in the heder and yeshivah, had studied the Talmud, the Cabbalah and Maimonides, but had had no opportunity to be taught a modern language. Without any teacher he had deciphered the German alphabet by means of adventurous combinations and immense labor; but he could not pronounce a German word correctly when he crossed the borders of Prussia. It took him a long time to learn German thoroughly. It took him even more time to adapt himself to the moderate mentality of his German contemporaries. For many years, his violent temper prevented him from concentrating upon the studies he had longed for. He provoked the indignation of his protector Moses Mendelssohn by his radical views and his licentiousness. He perplexed a Protestant minister who was to baptize him by his declaration that he regarded Judaism a religion superior to Christianity. After twelve years of wandering, Maimon anticipated many important views of post-Kantian philosophy, and influenced Fichte particularly. More than a century after Maimon's death, his thoughts became even more influential than during his lifetime. But great as was his philosophical thinking, his most interesting work is his autobiography which, in 1792, the German psychologist Karl Philipp Moritz edited under the title *Salomon Maimons Eigene Lebensgeschichte.* This book contains a charming description of Jewish life in Lithuania and a courageous vindication of rabbinic Judaism.

Maimonides (Moses ben Maimon)

(1135-1204)

Among the rabbis of the later Middle Ages and centuries thereafter, an adage was current, saying, "From Moses to Moses there is none like unto Moses." It means simply that Maimonides is to be regarded as the greatest figure in Jewish history since the man who delivered the Ten Commandments to the Jewish people. In fact, the spiritual development of Judaism up to the present age is incomprehensible without taking account of Maimonides' activities as a codifier, judge and commentator of the Bible and the Talmud. His *Mishneh Torah* (*Copy of the Law*) was the first systematic exposition of Jewish religion. His "articles of faith" are either quoted or poetically paraphrased in modern Jewish prayer books. The philosophical thoughts of Maimonides strongly influenced not only Jewish but also Islamic and Christian philosophers. The intention of his main work *Moreh Nebuchim* (*Guide of the*

Perplexed, in Arabic *Dalalat al Hairin*) was to prove that the teachings of Judaism are in harmony with the results of philosophical thinking, and that beyond that, they offer insight which reason alone cannot obtain. For this purpose, Maimonides prevalently used the works of Aristotle, and, to a lesser extent, those of Plato. Christian philosophers were eager to apply Maimonides' doctrine to the defense of their own religion or to the explanation of general principles. Thus did William of Auvergne, Alexander of Hales, Albertus Magnus, Meister Eckhart, Thomas Aquinas and, through him, all medieval and modern Thomists. The great jurist, Hugo Grotius, was inspired by Maimonides' views on the history of religion. Born in Cordova, Spain, Maimonides was forced to emigrate, at first to Morocco, then to Egypt where he earned his living by practicing medicine. In his medical treatises he anticipated modern discoveries concerning the affliction of the body by psychic factors, allergies, epilepsy, the nervous system and individual constitution. Almost all of his books were written in Arabic and shortly thereafter translated into Hebrew and Latin.

Malachi

One of the Minor Prophets, whose preachments paved the way for Nehemiah, 444 B.C.E.

Malkot

Flagellation.

Malshin

Informer.

Mamzer

Generally translated "bastard," this word has been established in Jewish law as referring to offspring of incest or adultery; such a one may not marry an Israelite woman, nor come into the congregation of the Lord.

Maneh

Biblical coin or weight.

Manna

Food, miraculously provided,

for the wandering Israelites (Exodus), which may have been an exudation from trees or a locust.

Manne, Mordecai Zvi

(1859-1886)

Poet, painter, of Wilna.

Maoz Tzur

Hymn sung on Chanukah.

Mapai

From "Mifleget Poale Eretz Israel"; Israel's dominant Socialist Labor party, organized by the Histadruth ha-Ovdim.

Mapam

Founded 1948, this leftish workers party in Israel has been frequently splintered; it has shown devotion to the Soviets.

Mapu, Abraham

(Lithuania, 1808–Germany, 1867)

Able Hebrew novelist, who wrote *Ahavat Zion (Love of Zion)*, *Ashmat Shomron (Sin of Samaria)*, and *Ayit Zavua (Painted Vulture)*.

Mar

Equivalent of "sir" in Aramaic.

Maria Hebrea

Alchemist and chemist of uncertain date; probably first century, Memphis.

Marranos

(Swine)

Name applied to Jews forced (anusim) to convert to Christianity in Spain, but who secretly observed their faith; the Inquisition (1478) was established to condemn and harass them.

Marriage

Jewish marriage may take place only between members of, or converts to, the faith—a provision maintained by all rabbis observing that tradition. Liberal Jews have deleted certain traditional rites, such as the ketubah (marriage contract) and the breaking of a glass by the groom.

Under traditional law, many deserted or widowed women cannot remarry (see AGUNAH and YEBAMAH); many days of the year are prohibited for marriages; the woman takes relatively passive part in ceremony. Liberal Judaism abolishes status of unmarriageable womanhood, eliminates all but Sabbath and high holidays as non-wedding days, and equalizes bride and groom at the ceremony; regarding divorce as a purely civil matter, it abrogates all religious divorce laws.

Marshall, Louis

(1856-1929)

Eminent American constitutional lawyer, who defended Jewish rights throughout the world, and was a leader in numerous Jewish organizations.

Marx, Karl

(1818-1883)

To the impact of Marx's doctrine on political and social ideas and the subsequent changes of social structure there is no parallel in the whole history of philosophy. Only religious reformers have produced similar changes. What distinguishes Marx from other philosophers who more or less deeply influenced political and social ideas is the simple fact that his teachings directly affected the mind of the masses of working people in various nations, not only by appealing to their material interests but even more so by imbuing them with an apparently imperturbable confidence in the absolute truth of his statements and predictions. The fundamental characteristic of Marx's doctrine is not his theory of the concentration of wealth in the hands of a few powerful capitalists, or the condemnation of the "exploitation of man by his fellow-man." These views are borrowed from Saint-Simon, Sismondi and Constantin Pecqueur. Nor is it his theory of class struggle, borrowed from French historians of his time, or his theory of surplus value, owed to English economists. What really dominates the unity of his thinking is his conception of history, according to which the forms of economic production determine the formation of human society and the consciousness of its members so that ideas, moral values, aesthetic standards, political and social concepts, educational and religious systems are to be conceived as produced by the economic situation. As long as the "ideological superstructure" remains in accordance with the conditions of economic production, civilization is healthy. But, since these conditions are changing more rapidly than the superstructure, cultural crises are unavoidable, and, when people, incapable of understanding the laws of history, resist the changes dictated by it, revolution becomes necessary. In his principal work *Das Kapital* (1867 and later) Marx developed his philosophy by applying it to modern economic life, demonstrating by a historico-sociological analysis of economics that that which he calls the *bourgeoisie* has accomplished its historical task by great performances but that it is not capable any longer of adapting itself to the changed conditions of production and must give room to the proletariat. Marx's gigantic stature was considerably dented by his anti-Semitic tendencies. Although himself a convert Jew, he persisted in public identifying Jews with money, banking, usury and materialism. In his pamphlet, *Zur Judenfrage,* he permits himself such statements as: "The basis of Judaism is selfishness. The only bond that ties Jews is the conservation of their property and their egotism." "The secular culture of the Jew is usury, his god—money. The emancipation from usury and money—that is, from realistic Judaism—would constitute the liberation of our time." This anti-Semitism blackened the socialistic movement of Europe from Proudhon to Stalin, and unfortunately has not yet ceased.

Mashal

Hebrew word meaning "allegory" or "fable."

Mashiach

Hebrew, "Messiah"; **Greek,** "Christos."

Masora

Tradition. Name for accepted (Masoretic) Bible text. Masoretes, headed by Ben Naphtali of the East and Ben Asher of the West, flourished sixth to ninth centuries.

Masoretic text

Bible text with added vowels.

Matriarchs

Sarah, Rebecca, Rachel, and Leah.

Mattathias

Heroic father of the Maccabees.

Matzah

Unleavened bread, eaten during Passover as remembrance of hasty departure from Egypt with unbaked dough.

Matzevah

Monument, tombstone; may be set thirty days after burial, though most mourners wait a year.

Mazal

"Luck"; as in "*mazal tov,*" "good luck." Mazal really means "planet."

Meat

By tradition must be of kosher animals, properly slaughtered; and kept apart from all dairy products or utensils.

Mechilta

Halakhic midrash to Exodus.

Mechutan

Connected through marriage.

Megillah

Roll; scroll of papyrus or leather. Word used alone means Book of Esther.

Meir

(2nd cent. B.C.E.)

Disciple of Rabbi Akiba, whose work in classifying Jewish law was continued by him. Later, sometimes confused with another rabbi, known as Meir Baal ha-Nes (miracle worker).

Melamed

Teacher. Term generally applied to old-time preceptor.

Melaveh Malkah

Meal eaten at close of Sabbath, often accompanied by speeches and entertainment for some good purpose. The phrase means "accompanying the Queen (Sabbath)." Also called Feast of King David, who, having been told he would die on the Sabbath, celebrated the conclusion of every Sabbath.

Menasseh ben Israel

(France, 1604–Netherlands, 1675)

It was an apocalyptic mystic, expecting the fulfillment of the messianic promises, who, in 1655, accomplished with extraordinary worldly ability the political and diplomatic task of securing permission for the Jews to settle again in England, from which they had been expelled in 1290. Menasseh ben Israel, who was able to put Oliver Cromwell in a mood favorable to his demands for readmission of the Jews to England, was also highly respected by Queen Christina of Sweden, had studied philosophy with Descartes, and his scholarship was exalted by men like Hugo Grotius and the learned theologian Johannes Buxtorff. Until the end of the 18th century, Menasseh ben Israel was considered a high authority in history, linguistics and theology by great scholars in Holland, England, France and Germany. Even greater was his influence with Christian mystics. He had studied the Cabbalah but was also well acquainted with orthodox rabbinic literature. His own writings, devoted to the vindication of Judaism, to its defense against accusations or to its reconciliation with philosophical and mystical doctrines, show him to be a versatile rather than a profound thinker. Among them, *Hope of Israel* (1650), dedicated to the Parliament of England, and *Vindication of the Jews* (1656) were written for political purposes, while *The Statue of Nebuchadnezzar* (1656), a commentary on Daniel's interpretation of the Babylonian king's dream, outlines a mystical philosophy of history. This book, when first printed, was decorated with four etchings by Rembrandt who, from 1645 on, was his intimate friend.

Mendele Mocher Sefarim

(1836-1917)

Pseudonym of Shalom Jacob Abramowitz, Lithuanian-born "grandfather of Yiddish literature." Helped revive Hebrew in literature, and transformed Yiddish into a literary language. (W) *Fathers and Sons, Little Menschel, Dobbin, Fische der Krummer, Wunschfinger, In the Days of Storm, Vale of Tears.*

Mendelssohn, Moses

(1729-1786)

In the late seventeenth century, Father Pierre Bonhours, a Jesuit and a refined art critic, published a pamphlet in which he held that a German could never be a poet or an artist, nor could he understand aesthetical problems and phenomena. Of course, the booklet aroused indignation in Germany, and provoked violent counterattacks. At that time, however, Frenchmen and Germans agreed that a Jew could never become integrated into modern culture, let alone contribute to its development. This opinion remained constant until, by 1755, the surprising news was spread in literary circles that there was in Berlin a Jew called Moses Mendelssohn who could not only speak and write German flawlessly but who could discuss philosophical and literary problems and was even esteemed by Lessing, the most feared German critic of his time, as an authority in aesthetics and psychology. Many otherwise independent thinkers would simply not believe that the news was true. Some of them went to Berlin in order to gaze in astonishment at such a curiosity. Then, for some years, even Mendelssohn's sincere admirers, such as Kant and Lessing, expressed doubts that he could continue to be devoted to German culture and at the same time remain loyal to Judaism. Later they recognized that he could do both.

Mendelssohn enriched descriptive psychology by his treatise on mixed sentiments. His essay on evidence in metaphysical sciences was awarded the prize by the Prussian Academy against his competitor, Immanuel Kant. His *Phaedon* (1767), defending the idea of the immortality of the soul, was a favorite book of German Jews and Christians alike for more than two generations. With his *Jerusalem* (1783), he deeply impressed Kant, who became convinced that Judaism was a true world religion. Mendelssohn also translated the Hebrew Bible into German and demanded civil rights for the Jews as well as the separation of Church and State. With him came the beginning of a new epoch in the history of the Jews, not only those of Germany. Still four decades after his death, hymns to his praise were sung by Christians and Jews united in their adherence to Mendelssohn's ideas. Lessing raised a poetic monument to his friend by using him as model for the hero of his drama *Nathan The Wise*.

Menorah

Seven-arm candelabrum in the Temple; symbol of Judaism, older than the Temple itself. For CHANUKAH (q.v.), eight-arm candle holder, with a ninth arm for the shammash (beadle).

Merkavah

Chariot; particularly divine chariot of Ezekiel's vision.

Meshumad

The Destroyed; religious renegade.

Met Mitzvah

A corpse without known relatives; it is commanded (mitzvah) that finder bury the body.

Metatron

The highest angel, identified with the archangel Michael, or with Enoch who was transformed into a heavenly being; a mystic figure.

Mezuzah

(Doorpost)

Wooden, metal, or plastic container for parchment containing Bible quotations, attached to right post of gates and doors in a Jewish household (Deut. 6:9). "And thou shalt write them upon the doorposts of thine house, and upon thy gates."

Micah

Prophet of messianic era.

Middat Harachamim

Character of mercy.

Midrash

(Exposition)

Homiletic commentary on the Biblical canon, divided into legal and ritual (Halakhah) and legendary, moralizing, folkloristic, and anecdotal (Haggadah) parts.

Midrash Rabbah

Large early collections of fact, anecdote, and preachment, on the Pentateuch and Five Scrolls.

Mikvah

Ritual bath, used mainly by married women after their periods, and by brides before nuptials; also for converts.

Milah

Circumcision (eighth day).

Milchig

Yiddish word referring to dairy foods, as opposed to *fleishig,* meat foods, under dietary regulations.

Minchah

Afternoon prayer; name of Temple sacrifice.

Minhag

(Custom)

Many customs, not antithetic to the principles of Jewish law, and practiced by large segments of the population, receive the power of law. Rabbi Moses Isserles interpolated many in the Shulchan Arukh; but these were binding on Ashkenazim and not on Sephardim. Some Chasidic customs are based on cabbalistic lore.

Minim

Sectaries; early Judeo-Christians.

Minyan

The minimum of ten Hebrew males over thirteen required for communal prayers.

Miriam

Sister of Moses; leader of Israelite women.

Miriam's Well

Legendary well accompanying the Hebrews on their trek through the desert.

Mishnah

(Teaching)

Basic compilation of legislation on Torah principles, concluded about 210 by Rabbi Judah the Prince. The lengthy disquisitions of the Talmud—Gemara—are based upon these brief and often cryptic paragraphs.

Mishpachah

Family.

Missionarizing

Not favored by Judaism, although *Ger Tzedek* (righteous convert) is received with open arms.

Mithnagged

(Opponent)

Antagonist of Chasidism.

Mixed Marriage

At all times and places a minority of Jews have married out of the faith; this has been strongly opposed by parents and leaders as a certain step to assimilation.

Mizrach

East. Prayers are directed toward Jerusalem.

Mizrachi

Religious Zionist movement founded in 1904; in 1957 united with Hapoel Hamizrachi into a unified religious Zionist organization, world and national.

Mizrachi Women

Religious Zionist organization.

Moab

Located on the east bank of the Dead Sea; closely related to the Israelites.

Moabite Stone

A stele recording King Mesha's battles with Israel, most important archaeologically. Stone is dated 9th cent. B.C.E. Destroyed by Arabs.

Mohel

Authorized functionary performing ritual circumcision.

Monarchy

Opposed by Samuel, Judge in Israel: "The king will take your sons, and appoint them unto him, for his chariots, and to be his horsemen; and they shall run before his chariots. . . . And he will take your fields, and your vineyards, and your olive-yards, and give them to his servants."

Monis, Judah

(1683-1764)

Born in Algiers, he was first a shochet with fair knowledge of Hebrew. Baptized 1722 at Cambridge, he was immediately thereafter appointed to Harvard faculty. Published first American Hebrew grammar, 1735. Wrote *Truth*, to prove Trinity out of Torah and Cabbalah.

Montefiore, Claude J. G.

(1858-1938)

London scholar, protagonist of Reform Judaism; wrote *The Bible for Home Reading, Aspects of Judaism, The Origin of Religion, Synoptic Gospels.*

Montefiore, Moses

(Leghorn, 1784–England, 1885)

British philanthropist who devoted most of his life and millions to assisting his fellow Jews everywhere, with special help for the Jews of Palestine. Made a knight and a baronet by Queen Victoria.

Morenu

(Our Teacher)

Honorary title bestowed upon Talmudic scholars.

Moses

Greatest Hebrew sage and lawgiver, presumed author of the Five Books bearing his name. He transformed his people into a Godly nation, with a new social order of justice, love of neighbor, and self-discipline. His impress is upon every part of the Pentateuch, and persists through the Bible. The final words of the Torah—ascribed to Joshua—declare: "So Moses, the servant of the Lord, died there in the land of Moab . . . and he was buried in the valley of Moab . . . and no man knoweth of his grave unto this day. . . . And there hath not arisen a prophet since in Israel like unto Moses whom the Lord knew soul to soul." Of the teachings of this greatest of the Hebrew sages, far too little has come down to us. Through the theological and legendary setting of the five sacred books attributed to him shines the indomitable light of a great Teacher imbued with the spirit and vision of a God-devoted life for his people under a social order founded on justice, neighborlove, and self-discipline. All available historical writings serve to emphasize the unique and precious personality of the profound lawmaker who carved in imperishable stone the very breath and beauty of the Lord's commandments. We do not know which of the legendary, historical, or ritualistic segments of the Mosaic books were written by this strange and princely shepherd, but dull must be the reader of the Bible who fails to detect the thunderous step of this benign and melancholy giant wandering through the sands of the desert.

Moses ben Nachman

(Gerona, 1194—Acre, 1270)

Spanish Talmudist and cabbalist who died in Palestine; also rabbi and physician. Public defender of Judaism against a renegade Jewish Dominican. Known as Nachmanides.

Motzi

Blessing over bread.

Mourning

There are many details in Jewish law concerning mourning ritual. The Kaddish is recited at daily services for eleven months by sons, and there are specific laws concerning the first seven days (SHIVAH) and thirty days (SHELOSHIM) of mourning. Liberals observe a seven-day period, with prayers on first three evenings, permit business activities during the days; and permit full grooming and personal care at all times.

Mukdam

Official of administrative board; Sephardic.

Music in worship

Traditional law permits only cantor and male choir; liberal practice admits instrumental music and mixed choir.

Mussaf

"Added" prayer service for Sabbaths and festivals, immediately following morning prayer.

N

Nabi, Navi

(pl. Neviim)

Prophet (one who proclaims or pronounces).

Nachmanides

See MOSES BEN NACHMAN.

Nagid

Prince; title of Jewish community head in medieval North Africa and Moorish Spain.

Nahum

Companion prophet to Jonah.

Names, additional

Sometimes given to very ill person (probably to confuse Angel of Death).

Naming child

At circumcision for boy; in synagogue for girl. ASHKENAZIC Jews do not use name of living parent or grandparent; but SEPHARDIM and liberal Jews do.

Naphtali

Son of Jacob and Bilhah; progenitor of one of the tribes of Israel.

Nasi

(Prince)

Title generally applied to head of the SANHEDRIN.

Nasi, Joseph

(ca. 1515-1579)

MARRANO who was made Duke of Naxos by Turkish sultan, and used his power to assist European Jews.

Nathan

Prophet who lived during the reign of David.

National Council of Jewish Women

108,000 members throughout the United States, aiding and educating the young, helping the aged and the immigrant; also sponsors programs for Israelis and other foreign Jewish communities.

National Council of Young Israel

Group engaged in traditional religious and cultural practices, their spread and intensification.

National Federation of Temple Brotherhoods; Sisterhoods

Affiliated with the Union of American Jewish Congregations.

National Jewish Welfare Board

Central agency of Jewish Community Center activity, engaged also in various cultural activities and welfare of service men.

Nazirite

One separated; ascetic who vowed to abstain from wine, haircutting, touching the dead, and other restraints. Where no time was specified the vow held good for thirty days.

Nehardea

One of the earliest centers of Babylonian Judaism.

Nehemiah

("Solace of God")

Cupbearer to Artaxerxes, who was governor in Jerusalem fifth century B.C.E. Served with Ezra in Judaic revival. Bible book, allied with Book of Ezra.

Neilah

(Closing of Gates)

Final service of Yom Kippur.

Nekamah

Revenge.

Neo-Orthodoxy

The revival of traditional Jewish observance by Rabbi Samson Raphael Hirsch.

Ner Tamid

(Eternal Light)

A lamp or other illumination always burning before the Holy Ark, symbolizing the eternal presence of God.

Nevelah

Carcass of animal not slaughtered according to ritual, or otherwise ritually defective.

New Testament

Reflects the depth of Hebrew wisdom literature, despite its un-Hebraic theology and unfeasible ethics. ("I come not to destroy the Law, but to fulfill it.")

New Year

(Rosh ha-Shanah)

First day of month Tishri. "Day of Memorial" in Bible—man remembers Creation and the Creator. SHOFAR, traditionally unadorned ram's horn, is sounded: there are three kinds of blasts, single, triple, and sevenfold. Many unique hymns and poems are recited; best known is *Unetaneh Tokef* ("Let us proclaim the mighty holiness of this day"), by Rabbi Amnon of Mainz, martyred by the Germans. One is permitted to prostrate oneself before the Lord on this day. It is the beginning of the Ten Days of Penitence, ending Yom Kippur.

Niddah

Ritually unclean woman.

Niddui

Mild form of excommunication.

Niger, Samuel

(1884-1955)

Russian-born Yiddish writer who became leading Yiddish literary critic in America, with special interest in its aesthetics and sociology.

Niggun

Liturgical chant.

Nimrod

First hunter in Bible (Gen. x).

Nisan

First (springtime) month of year, during which Passover falls.

Nissuin

Taking in marriage; the ceremony.

Noachian Laws

The seven commandments which are obligatory on all men regardless of belief. They are: prohibition to eat flesh of a living creature, blasphemy, robbery, murder, paganism, perversion and the precept to do justice. Talmudic scholars have seen in them a road to religious tolerance.

Noachides

Descendants of Noah.

Noah, Mordecai Emanuel

(1785-1851)

American diplomat and dramatist who attempted to establish a Jewish city of refuge on Grand Island, New York.

Nordau, Max

(Budapest, 1849–Paris, 1923)

Philosopher, dramatist, novelist, essayist, physician; Zionist leader; wrote *Conventional Lies of Our Civilization, The Real Country of the Billions, From Kreml to Alhambra, Soap Bubbles, Paris Under the Third Republic, Paradoxes, The Maladies of the Century, Degeneration, Dr. Kohn.*

Numbers

Fourth Book of Moses. Forty years of wandering through desert and wilderness, and in enemy lands.

Numerals

None in Biblical antiquity, Hebrew letters being used as figures and numbers spelled out in Bible.

Numerus clausus

(Latin)

Limited number of Jews admitted to schools of higher education; still operative in Soviet Union.

Nusach

Type of liturgical melodies at services.

O

Obadiah

Shortest prophetic book; foretells destruction of Edomites, descendants of Esau.

Olah

Burnt offering in Temple.

Olam ha-Dimyon

World of Illusion, to which all the souls of the vain depart.

Olam ha-Tohu

World of Confusion; temporary domicile of the soul prior to redemption.

Old Testament

Common term for Hebrew Bible—39 books (24 by rabbinical reckoning). Parts: Pentateuch, Prophets, Hagiographa (Holy Writings). Composed over period of a thousand years; canon established at Jamnia about 100 C.E., with apocryphal works (mainly in Greek) rejected by Palestinians, but accepted by Alexandrian Jews and those who prepared the Septuagint. Written in Hebrew, with some Aramaic. Many portions, even in historical books, are poetic. Translated into over a thousand tongues and dialects. Term first used by Paul of Tarsus, but without validity in Jewish thought, which knows this literature only as the Bible.

Omer

(Sheaf)

The period of fifty days counted between Passover and Shavuoth; traditionally a mourning period, when no one—except on Lag ba-Omer—may wed, cut his hair, or otherwise engage in affairs of public joy or vanity.

Onan

Mourner (between death and burial).

Oneg Shabbat

Joy of Sabbath; social gathering on the day.

Onkelos

Second-century teacher and convert, to whom is ascribed the Aramaic translation of the Bible.

Opatoshu, Joseph

(1888——)

Russian-born Yiddish novelist, who in the U.S. wrote mainly about life in the Old Country.

Oppenheim, Moritz Daniel

(1801-1882)

Popular German painter of Jewish life and portraits of the great.

Organ

Introduced in Reform Temples by Israel Jacobson (Berlin, 1815); later accepted by many conservative synagogues. Traditional Jews have prohibited instrumental music at synagogue services since destruction of Temple.

Orlah

Foreskin; first three years of fruit from trees, which may not be eaten.

ORT

Organization for Rehabilitation by Training; founded 1880 for developing Jewish industry and agriculture.

Orthodox Judaism

Acceptance of the total body of Jewish law, from Pentateuch

through its faithful interpreters. The latter include the Talmud, the Mishneh Torah of Maimonides, and the Shulchan Arukh code of Joseph Caro. Though traditional Judaism has forgone many observances in the diaspora (and even now in Israel), it has never disclaimed their validity. Its rabbis did not seek to adjust Judaism to its milieus, but to apply the law to even the most complicated new circumstances; the Karaites (q.v.) sought complete return to Pentateuchal law as opposed to the Talmud and later writings. The Orthodox have looked upon Hebrew as a sacred language, consider Moses the ultimate authority over matters mundane and spiritual, and have ever held the messianic hope of a return to the Holy Land. The term "orthodox" arose after the emancipation that followed the French and American Revolutions. Though Reform and Conservative Judaism have modified traditional observance, most of the world's Jews remain Orthodox.

P

Palestine

Name from "Philistine." Arab name, Filastin. Biblical Canaan, land of two kingdoms, Israel and Judah (also known as Judea). After 1948 War of Liberation, called Israel; citizens, Israelis.

Parashah

Each section of the Pentateuch read on Sabbaths and festivals in synagogue.

Parnas

Lay head of a congregation.

Parokhet

Decorative curtain hanging before Holy Ark.

Parush

Separatist in religious matters; monkish.

Passover

This spring festival, beginning NISSAN 15 and continuing for seven or eight days, commemorates the Exodus from Egypt, with other national, religious, and agricultural significances. No leaven may be eaten; matzot replace bread. All year-round dishes and utensils are replaced. The ceremonial commemorative meal, seder, is conducted on the first or both first and second nights.

Patriarchs

(Avot)

Abraham, Isaac, Jacob.

Peace

(Shalom)

Underlying principle of Jewish life and teaching: "Seek peace and pursue it." Greeting and farewell in Hebrew are both "Shalom."

Pentecost

See SHAVUOTH.

Peretz, Isaac Leib

(1851-1915)

Classical Yiddish writer of verse, drama, and short stories; many of last appear in anthologies in modern languages. Polish; radical in thought. (W) *Dybbuk, The Crazy Man, The Golem, The Shtreimel, Meisselbach, The Golden Chain, The Night in the Old Market.*

Pesach Sheni

Second Passover, observed a month late by travelers who could not sacrifice the paschal lamb.

Pesha

Deliberate sin or crime.

Pesikta

Book of Haggadic discourses for festivals and special Sabbaths.

Pesuke d'Zimrah

Psalms and prayers introducing morning worship.

Petichah

Opening of the Ark as part of service.

Peyot

"Corners" of the beard; earlocks left uncut by very pious Jews.

Pfefferkorn, Johann

(1469-1521?)

Apostate Moravian Jew who violently assailed the Jewish faith, and would have succeeded in having all Jewish books in the kingdom except the Bible destroyed were it not for the intercession of Reuchlin and other Christian scholars.

Pharisees

(Perushim—separatists)

After the Maccabeans, this group, the Jewish majority, preached adherence to religious practices (with permitted legal modifications), and observance of the Oral Law. They were opposed by the limited, aristocratic Sadducees. Pharisees democratized ritual and reduced influence of priestly caste. They brought Judaism closer to the Jewish home. They generally believed in an afterlife. There is no truth whatever in Christian and other strictures against the Pharisees, who represented the finest traditions of their people and of human morals.

Philo Judaeus

(About 25 B.C.E.—before 50 C.E.)

The importance of Philo to the history of philosophy is incomparably greater than the power of his personality or the relevance of his personal thinking. For about seventeen centuries his example was, consciously and unconsciously, followed by all European thinkers, notwithstanding their differences, no matter whether they were nominalists or realists, idealists or naturalists, orthodox or heretics, and today Catholic Neo-Scholasticism is still following him, not to mention his influence on Islamic and Jewish philosophy. Philo was the first thinker to introduce into epistemology, metaphysics, physics and ethics the problem of reconciling speculative thought with the data of Biblical revelation; or, rather, he established these data, especially with characteristics of God, Man and Nature as the perfect truth with which the philosopher had to harmonize the results of his thinking. In this way, Philo created a spiritual situation, completely unknown in pagan Greek philosophy, which had not to regard Sacred Scripture as the standard and source of truth. The impact of the belief in the pagan gods on philosophical thought had only occasionally caused conflicts and had become negligible. As a positive support of thinking, as a source of knowledge, the belief in the pagan gods was of no account even when some philosophers used the gods as symbols of forces which were comprehended by speculative methods. Philo initiated a new era in the history of philosophy, the earliest documents of which can be noted in the Gospel of St. John. Its great development begins with the Fathers of the Church, comprises the whole Middle Ages and part of modern times, Descartes included. It was Spinoza, a Jew like Philo, who removed Biblical revelation from the realm of philosophy. But, unlike Spinoza, Philo, a contemporary of Jesus and Saint Paul, remained a faithful, professing Jew. He devoted the main part of his life to the interpretation of the Pentateuch and to the defense of the Jewish faith against attacks on the part of gentile critics by explaining the essence of Judaism from the historical, philosophical, ethical and juridical points of view. When he was elected leader of a Jewish embassy to Rome in 40 C.E., he tried to defend his coreligionists against the arbitrary power of Emperor Caligula. Although Philo borrowed much from Greek philosophers, his system deviates widely from purely Greek lines. It is the doctrine of monotheistic mysticism, teaching that the human mind is capable, by intuition, not by reasoning, to apprehend God's existence but not His nature. In this way, Philo was the first to outline a psychology of faith. (W) *Legatio ad Caium, De Specialibus Legibus, Josephus.*

Phylacteries

(Greek, "amulet")

Leather bands and small cases with parchment strips with Mosaic extracts (Ex. 13:1-10, 11-16; Deut. 6:4-9; 11:13-21), worn on forehead and left arm at weekday morning prayers: "And thou shalt bind them for a sign upon thine hand, and they shall be for frontlets between thine eyes." Called TEFILLIN.

Pidyon ha-Ben

Redemption of the first-born;

ceremony conducted thirty full days after birth, redeeming first-born, if male, from service to the Almighty, as prescribed when the Temple stood.

Pilegesh

Concubine.

Pilpul

The dialectics whereby Talmudic matters were discussed and harmonized; probably from a word meaning "research" or "judgment."

Pinsker, Leon

(1821-1891)

Early political Zionist; physician; author of *Auto-Emancipation,* declaring Jewish nationalism the only antidote to anti-Semitism.

Pinski, David

(Russia, 1872—)

Foremost dramatist in Yiddish. Born in Ukraine, studied in Vienna. Under influence of I. L. Peretz in Warsaw, attached self to Jewish Socialist Movement. Came to U.S.A. in 1899, emigrated to Israel in 1950. Wrote historical romances, realistic novels of Jewish life, and plays: *The Treasure, King David and His Wives, The Final Balance.*

Piyyutim

Liturgical poems with Biblical or religious motifs added to Jewish services, particularly on high holidays. Some of the great liturgical poets are Solomon ibn Gabirol, Moses ibn Ezra, and Judah Halevi.

Poalei Agudat Israel

Workers' section of the Agudat Israel party of Israel.

Pogrom

Murderous assault on Jewish community.

Pope, Jewish

Anaclete II (1130-1138).

Porging

Removal of prohibited fat and back veins from kosher animals.

Posekim

(Deciders)

Post-Talmudic authorities on Jewish law and practice. The earliest were called Kadmonim; these end with tenth-century Saadia Gaon. Then came the Rishonim (first), up to 15th century, including Alfasi and Maimonides. Those of 16th to 18th centuries, Acharonim (last), included Jacob ben Asher and Moses Isserles.

Poshea Yisrael

Offender against Israel.

Prayer shawl

To cover eyes and head of worshiper to avoid distraction. See TALLITH.

Precepts

Maimonides reckons the divine precepts or commands (MITZVOT) of the TORAH as 613, including positive and negative commands.

Promised Land

Canaan, then Palestine, now Israel; assured as possession of Abraham and his descendants.

Progressive Party

Political party in Israel, of middle and working class membership, with liberal tendencies, but non-socialist.

Prophets

Three "Major" and twelve "Minor" Prophets, ranging from 870 to 440 B.C.E., covering eras before, during, and after exile.

Prosbul

Since the Bible ordained release of all debts on the sabbatical year, rendering loans difficult, Hillel instituted this method of protecting creditors through a special court procedure.

Proselyte

(Ger)

Judaism does not proselytize, but accepts the honest *ger* (original meaning, "stranger, sojourner"). There are variations: the *ger toshav*, who accepts monotheism and the Noachide laws, and who receives courtesies and privileges; the *gere tzedek,* full converts, in all respects to be considered Jews; and *gere sheker,* who declare themselves full converts for ulterior motives.

Protocols of the Wise Men (Elders) of Zion

A book, repeatedly proven a forgery, used by Hitler and other anti-Semites to show an international Jewish organization determined on altering all civilization in favor of Jewish rule.

Proverbs: Ecclesiastes

Companion works of wisdom in Bible, both ascribed to Solomon.

Psalms

In general attributed to King David; some are directly credited to his songmaster Asaph; two to Solomon; Psalm 90 to Moses. Called TEHILLIM, "Songs of Praise."

Purim

(Lots)

Festival of Lots, Adar 14. Celebrates rescuing of Jews from destruction at hands of premier of Persia, Haman—who cast lots to determine day of holocaust. Esther, chosen queen by Ahasuerus, saved her people; the Book of Esther is read twice on Purim. It is a happy day, when gifts and alms are given (*mishloach manot*). Masquerades, plays, and general jollity mark the day.

R

Rabbi

Literally, "my master," "my teacher." Talmudic scholars held the title, but earned their livelihoods through secular occupations. Later specialized religious leaders arose; they were also communal arbiters and judges; today rabbis function very much like clergymen of other faiths, providing pastoral guidance and supervision of religious ceremonies. However, the rabbi in no way differs basically from the layman as to religious duties and responsibilities. No intermediary between man and God, he still represents the chain of tradition through all the generations of Israel.

Rachel (Blaustein)

Born in Russia 1890, this muse of Jewish folklore and other Judaic themes, died 1931 in Tel Aviv. Her chief work is called *Shirat Rachel.*

Ralbag

See GERSONIDES.

Ramban

See MOSES BEN NACHMAN.

Rapoport, Solomon Judah Loeb

(Lwow, 1790–Prague, 1867)

Rabbi of Prague, who helped establish Jewish science; author of uncompleted dictionary of Judaism.

Rashbam

Samuel ben Meir, grandson of Rashi (1085-1174), who also wrote Biblical commentaries.

Rashi

(Solomon ben Isaac, 1040-1105)

This scholar of Troyes is the world's greatest commentator; his notes on Bible and Talmud are virtually a part of the text.

Rav

1.Rabbi. 2. See ABBA AREKA.

Rechabites

Kenite tribe, nomadic, shunning house and farm; ascetics, praised for their simple modes by Jeremiah.

Reconstructionism

A modern movement, founded by Professor Mordecai M. Kaplan, attempting to unify the Jewish community and treating Judaism as a civilization.

Reform Judaism

Movement begun in nineteenth century to alter traditional Jewish practices (changes since accepted in part by Conservative Judaism), such as doffing of hats, mixed choir and organ music, equality of women at services and as synagogue functionaries, use of the vernacular, reducing festival days; as well as the now commonly practiced development of educational principles, synagogue financing through membership dues, permanent national religious bodies. From 2,700 families in 1830, the movement had grown to 170,000 families by 1955. Accepts as binding only the ethical laws of the Bible, rejecting other laws, rites and ceremonies unless designed to "elevate and sanctify our lives."

Refuge, Cities of

(Are Miklat)

Six cities in ancient Israel set aside for unintentional murderers seeking to escape blood avengers.

Rehoboam

King Solomon's son. In his reign (930 B.C.E.-913 B.C.E.) the Kingdom split into two parts. He remained ruler over the southern part called Judah.

Reinach, Salomon

(1858-1932)

Classical archaeologist; religious philosopher; vice-president of Alliance Israélite Universelle.

Reisen, Abraham

(d. 1953)

Born in Russia 1876, this popular Yiddish poet and story writer continued his work in the U.S. 1908. Prominent Socialist.

Religion

(Latin, "binding")

Chain of tradition binding a group.

Repentance

(Teshuvah, "Return")

Major Jewish principle; marked during Ten Days of Penitence, covering Rosh ha-Shanah and Yom Kippur.

Resh Galutha

Head of the Exile; leader of Babylonian Jewish community.

Reshit Chokhmah

Beginning of wisdom.

Reshut

Power; authority; permissiveness.

Responsa

(Teshuvot)

Legal opinions (replies) written for individual or communal inquirers by eminent Talmudists

Resurrection

See: IMMORTALITY.

Reuben

One of the sons of Jacob; his descendants form one of the tribes of Israel.

Reubeni, David

Messianic pretender of the sixteenth century, of many wanderings and stratagems; died prisoner of Spanish Inquisition.

Reuchlin, Johannes von

(1455-1522)

German Christian humanist and defender of Judaism against attacks of apostate Johann Pfefferkorn.

Revisionism

A Zionist movement organized by Vladimir Jabotinsky, advocating an enlarged Israel on both sides of Jordan, and more militancy for Jewish rights.

Ribalow, Menachem

Russian-born (1896-1953) Hebraist and writer, who came to U.S. in 1921, edited *Hadoar* and various works, and served as head of the Histadrut Ivrit.

Rieti, Moses

(1388-1460)

Poet, physician, philosopher, historian, chief rabbi of Rome; wrote *Mikdash Meat,* in imitation of Dante.

Rishonim

See POSEKIM.

Rishut

Evil—generally referring to anti-Semitism.

Ritualism

Basic principle of Judaism, which is a religion of observance and works, as opposed to basic Christianity, a religion of faith.

Rosenfeld, Morris

(Poland, 1862—New York, 1917)

First Yiddish poet of distinction in U.S. (W) *Die Glocke, Blumenkette, Yiddische Mai, Lieder Buch.*

Rosenzweig, Franz

(1886-1929)

Shortly before the outbreak of the First World War, a young German scholar of Jewish origin, who had become renowned because of his epoch-making discovery of the earliest outline of German idealism and his acute investigation of the relations between Schelling and Hegel, intended to embrace Christianity. But before making the decisive step he thought it would be appropriate to know what he intended to abandon. He therefore began to study Judaism, and subsequently became resolved not only to remain a Jew, but also to devote his life to the elaboration of a new conception of Judaism, based upon historical, linguistic, and philosophical research, and aimed at a moral and spiritual rejuvenation of his fellow Jews. The first fruit of these efforts was the book *Der Stern der Erloesung* (*Star of Salvation*), written during the war in the trenches and edited posthumously in 1930. Rosenzweig's vindication of Judaism is anything but polemical toward Christianity. He is opposed to atheism and irreligion, but his historical consciousness prevents him from attacking, even from disputing, any religious tradition or any living faith. On the contrary, he encouraged his closest friend and first cousin to embrace Christianity rather than to live apart from any religious community. Although opposed to Jewish nationalism, Rosenzweig thinks that Jewish religion concerns only born Jews, and without any concession to racialism, founds his philosophy of history upon the fact that the Jews form a cultural unit with a common history and certain relatively constant characteristics. He even maintains that only the Jews, by virtue of being such a unit, can have a genuine philosophy of history in which their fate, regarded as a unit, is the decisive factor. The historical aspect is also of primary importance to Rosenzweig's philosophy of religion which, notwithstanding the tensions between religion and civilization, is at the same time a philosophy of culture.

Rosh Chodesh

"Head of the Month."

Rosh ha-Shanah

See NEW YEAR.

Rosh Yeshivah

Head of a Talmudic institution.

Rossi, Azariah

(ca. 1513-1578)

Critic of Hebraic and other literatures whose chief work on Jewish chronology and archaeology is *Meor Enayim (Light of the Eyes)*.

Roth, Leon

(b. 1896, London)

Philosopher who teaches at Hebrew University. Author of *Spinoza, Descartes, and Maimonides.*

Rothschild

This is the famed banking family, whose financial activities began in Frankfort with Mayer Amschel Rothschild and spread through Europe.

Ruach ha-Kodesh

The indwelling Spirit which gives life and inspiration to man; Talmudically, one of the ten things God created on the first day.

Runes, Dagobert David

Contemporary Jewish philosopher. *Dictionary of Philosophy, Letters to My God, On the Nature of Man, Of God, the Devil and the Jews, A Book of Contemplation.*

Russia

Archcenter of anti-Semitism, under both Czars and Soviets. Except for Hitler, more Jews were executed by Stalin than by any other modern group. Though Lenin outlawed anti-Semitism, in 1924 it was brought back in virulent form by Stalin, his successor. The Soviets have masked their Jew hatred by calling victims Trotzkyite, Titoite, cosmopolite, Zionist, and other epithets. The czarist and Hitler bugaboo of a Jewish conspiracy to dominate the world (through the "Elders of Zion") has been employed by Stalinites and their successors. In the late twenties Stalin established a huge Siberian ghetto in Biro-Bidjan, to lure the Jews out of Europe; but also poured into the territory known anti-Semites such as Cossacks and Tartars. Today there is no Jewish publication or cultural center in Russia. Of all religions, Judaism is under the strictest interdiction. Only a show rabbi and show synagogue are permitted in Moscow. In Russia Zionism is anathema; the Arabic haters of Israel are aided and idealized.

Ruth

Pastoral idyl of David's great-grandmother.

S

Saadia

(892-942)

Until Saadia began to formulate his ideas, the spiritual atmosphere of his times had been, as one of his contemporaries complained, as follows: "Muslims, Jews, Christians and Magicians, they all are walking in error and darkness. There are two kinds of people left in the world: the one group is intelligent but lacking in faith, the other has faith but is lacking in intelligence." And so it became Saadia's purpose to teach not only his Jewish coreligionists but also Islamic and Christian thinkers that faith is not opposed to reason but only to pseudo-reason. Born in Egypt, and educated as well in all branches of Arabian culture as in Biblical and Talmudic scholarship, Saadia went to Palestine, and then to Babylonia. There he accomplished his great work which became the foundation of Jewish philosophy and science. Acquainted with Greek philosophy, the various formulations of the Christian dogma, the doctrines of the Manicheans, of Zoroaster and even with the philosophy of India, Saadia developed the idea that Judaism is compatible with all truth, whatever its source. In his explanation of the nature of religion, the character of man and the way of conceiving God, Saadia criticized Plato's cosmology and refuted gnostic doctrines.

He tried to reconcile the idea of freedom of man with that of the all-embracing foreknowledge of God. Saadia was also a learned mathematician and a trained philologist, and he composed the first Hebrew dictionary as well as the first Jewish prayer book. (W) *Sefer Emunot ve-De'ot* (*Book of Faith and Doctrines*).

Sabbath

(Rest)

Seventh day of the week; last day of Creation in Genesis. Day of rest and reminder of divine justice on earth. The day is ushered in when the housewife lights candles a half-hour or more before sunset. An important part of the evening prayer is *Lechah Dodi* ("Come, my friend, to meet the bride"), by Solomon Alkabez (sixteenth century), in which the Sabbath is likened to a new bride.

Sabbath observance

No work is permitted except that connected with worship or preservation of life and health; there is no handling of money, no artificial mode of communication, no participation in labor or entertainment performance. Reform permits all forms of communication, and honors Sabbath by worship only.

Sabbath of Sabbaths

Yom Kippur.

Sabbath Queen, Escort of

See MELAVEH MALKAH.

Sabbatical Year

The Mosaic Code sought to emphasize man's responsibility to his neighbors by commanding that on the seventh year the land must lie fallow for the sake of the poor, and all debts had to be remitted. In modified forms this general mode of life was observed into the Middle Ages.

Saboraim

"Those who reflect," who in the sixth century gave definite form to the TALMUD.

Sabra

(Cactus)

Israel native (the cactus has

rough exterior, and sweet interior).

Sackcloth

Used as garment of mourning; cf. "sackcloth and ashes."

Sacrifices

Offering of animals and grain discontinued after destruction of the Temple, except among sectaries such as the Samaritans.

Sadducees

(from Zadok, a priestly family)

Party of aristocratic priestly group during time of the Second Temple. Opposed Pharisees, who advocated democratization, and liberation of Jewish life from control of priests. They denied the afterlife, validity of the Oral Law, and the need for services outside the Temple.

Sagerin

"Speaker" (German) who read the portion and the prayers for her fellow women at old synagogues.

Sahula, Isaac ben Solomon

Thirteenth-century Spanish fabulist and commentator; author of *Meshal Hakadmoni* (*Fable of the Ancient*) in verse.

Salome Alexandra

Queen of Judah, wife of Alexander Jannai, who helped her brother, Simeon ben Shetach, organize school of Hebrew learning, 76 B.C.E.

Samael

("Venom of God")

Angel of death; angel of evil; prince of the demons.

Samaria

Capital of Israel, northern kingdom.

Samaritans

Sect originating in Samaria, North Israel. Mixed population. Refused participation in rebuilding Temple by Zerubbabel, they made Mount Gerizim their holy place; they sacrifice thereon every Passover. Observe only Pentateuchal laws. Small in numbers, the sect now lives in Nablus, Jordan.

Samson

Last of the Judges; strong man who was betrayed to the Philistines by Delilah.

Samuel

Prophet who succeeded the Judges and anointed Saul as first king of Israel; Biblical book bearing his name is in two parts.

Samuel ben Abba

(Mar Samuel) (180-257)

Leading Babylonian amora, head of Nahardea academy and associated with Rav in rendering Babylonian scholarship independent of that in Palestine, third century.

Samuel ha-Levi ben Joseph ibn Nagdela

(993-1055)

This Spanish scholar, called Samuel ha-Nagid, of wide Jewish and general learning, became vizier to caliph of Malaga. Among his works are poetic simulations of Psalms, Proverbs, and Ecclesiastes: *Ben Tehillim* and *Ben Kohelet.*

Samuel, Herbert

(Liverpool, 1870—)

Viscount; philosopher and statesman who was first High Commissioner of Palestine (1920); author of philosophical and political works, including *Philosophy and the Ordinary Man* and *In Search of Reality.*

Sandek

Godfather who holds infant on his knees at circumcision.

Sanhedrin

Supreme Jewish court; in Jerusalem, after exile to middle of second century C. E. Great civil authority; required Roman approval for death penalty. Great Sanhedrin in Jerusalem had 71 members, all scholars and sages; lesser courts had 23.

Saragossi, Joseph

(15th-16th centuries)

Talmudic and cabbalistic authority, who helped make his home, Safed, the center of Jewish cabbalism.

Saul

First king of Israel (eleventh century B.C.E.). Anointed by prophet Samuel. Carried on long feud with David, who was to become his successor. Died in battle at Gilboa.

Schechter, Solomon

(1850-1915)

This Rumanian-born scholar taught at Cambridge, then became president of the Jewish Theological Seminary of America. His first fame came when he discovered the original text of *Ben Sira* and other works in the Cairo Genizah (depository of discarded Hebrew works). His editing and writing included three *Studies in Judaism, Some Aspects of Rabbinic Theology, Documents of Jewish Sectaries, Saadyana, Midrash ha-Gadol to Genesis, A Glimpse of the Social Life of the Jews.*

Schreiber (Sofer), Moses

(Frankfurt, 1763—Pressburg, 1839)

Noted rabbinical scholar who founded academy at Pressburg. Author of *Chatam Sofer.*

Schulman, Samuel

(Russia, 1864-1955)

Russian-born American Reform rabbi and scholar.

Science of Judaism

"*Wissenschaft des Judentums*"—term coined by Leopold Zunz (1794-1886), German rabbi who organized a society to advance scientific study of his faith.

Scribes

(Soferim)

Copyists of the Torah and other portions of the Bible, beginning with Ezra; they also modified and commented on the text in order to ameliorate the harshness of some of the precepts.

Scroll of the Law

See SEFER TORAH.

Seder

See PASSOVER.

Seder Olam

Ancient work of unknown authorship, describing Biblical and later events, to second century.

Sefer

Book.

Sefer Torah

Handwritten scroll of the Pentateuch.

Sefer Yetzirah

See CABBALAH.

Sefiroth

The ten emanations of cabbalistic doctrine.

Segan

Chief, superior officer; man who distributes synagogue honors.

Sela'

Biblical coin or weight equal to one sacred or two common shekels.

Selah

A final word in Psalms and Habakkuk, probably meaning a musical pause; in the Talmud, "to all eternity."

Selichot

Penitential prayers recited on the days preceding Rosh ha-Shanah and during the Ten Days of Penitence.

Semichah

Ordination of a rabbi by "laying on of hands." Laying hands on head of sacrificial animal.

Semites

Presumed descendants of Shem, Noah's oldest son. Jews and Arabs so designated.

Semitic Languages

One of the largest and best recorded groups. Hebrew is a Semitic tongue; there are groupings known as Accadian (Babylonian-Assyrian); Canaanitic

(Phoenician, Punic, Moabite); Aramaean (North Semitic); South Semitic (North Arabian, South Arabian, Abyssinian, and also Egyptian and Coptic).

Semukhin

Adjacent, connected; applied to Talmudic relating of Biblical passages together in text.

Sepharad

Spain.

Sephardi

Descriptive title applying mainly to Iberian Jews and their descendants, largely centered on the Mediterranean. Origin of word vague (Obadiah 20).

Sephiroth

See CABBALAH.

Septuagint

According to several writers of the era, King Ptolemy Philadelphus of Egypt had Bible translated into popular Greek, second century B.C.E. There were 72 translators, who completed the project in 70 days, no text differing from the others. However, part of the work is not literal.

Seven Shepherds

Abraham, Isaac, Jacob, Joseph, Moses, Aaron, and David, who are welcomed as guests in the Sukkah.

Sforno, Obadiah

(1475-1550)

Italian physician, commentator, philosopher, who taught Reuchlin Hebrew.

Shaatnez

Biblically prohibited fabric of wool and linen (Lev. 19:19).

Shabbas goy

A non-Jew hired to perform essential work forbidden to Jews on Sabbaths—generally to kindle or extinguish lights.

Shabbat ha-Gadol

Great Sabbath, immediately before Passover.

Shabbat Shirah

Sabbath of Song, when the song of the Israelites at the Red Sea is read (Ex. 15).

Shabbat Shuvah

The Sabbath falling during the Ten Days of Penitence, between Rosh ha-Shanah and Yom Kippur.

Shabbetai Zevi

(1626-1676)

Most influential of medieval false Messiahs; though excommunicated, became wandering leader of multitudes who accepted him at his own divine appraisal. But when given choice of punishment or conversion, he accepted Mohammedanism.

Shacharit

Morning prayer. From Hebrew for "dawn."

Shadchan

Marriage broker.

Shaddai

"Master," "Destroyer"; a name of God.

Shalach Manoth

Sending of gifts, particularly at Purim.

Shalom Alechem

Hebrew greeting—"Peace be with you."

Shalom, S.

(Galicia, 1904—)

One of most authentic Israeli poets, whose book *Mipanim el Panim* won the Bialik prize of 1941.

Shalosh Seudot

The three festive meals prescribed for the Sabbath.

Shamir

In Jewish legendry a worm that can split rocks and iron by its glance; said to have done the work of prohibited iron tools in erecting the Temple.

Shammai

Palestinian tanna, 30 B.C.E., known for his opposition to the generally milder judgments of Babylonian-born Hillel.

Shammash

Sexton, servant; extra Chanukah candle used to light the others.

Shass

Abbreviation of *Shishah Sedarim,* six orders of the Mishnah and Talmud (Zeraim, Moed, Nashim, Nezikin, Kodoshim, Tohorot). The word is used to designate the entire Talmud (63 volumes).

Shavuoth

Feast of Weeks (Pentecost) and time of Giving of the Law; hence liberal Jews have instituted confirmation ceremonies on that festival.

Shechitah

Ritual slaughter.

She'elot u-Teshuvot

Questions and Responses; responses to queries on matters of Jewish law, by rabbis and sages.

Shehecheyanu

A blessing—"Who hath kept us alive"—to this time; recited when one takes possession of or begins something new, including the holidays. It is used frequently at the time of other special events.

Shekel

(Weight)

Silver coin in Israel from days of Maccabees. Half a coin was prescribed Temple contribution in Bible. Membership in World Zionist Organization today symbolically costs a shekel.

Shekhinah

The Divine (Indwelling) Presence in the world and its creatures.

Shelamim

Peace offerings in the Temple.

Sheliach Tzibbur

Representative of the community; today used to denote the cantor who repeats the services. Originally an office exercised by priest or rabbi, except those unable to read Hebrew, who said nothing but "Amen."

Sheloshet Yeme Hagbalah

"Three days of setting bounds" at Mount Sinai, when the people were not permitted to approach (Ex. 19:12).

Sheloshim

Thirty days of full mourning; number of days on which prayers are said by mourner who is not a child of the deceased.

Shem ha-Kodesh

Religious first name. See CHILD NAMING.

Shem ha-Meforash

The "explicit name" used in Jewish literature for the unexpressed Jahweh.

Shema

Cardinal principle of Judaism, recited at daily prayers, and before death (Deut. 6:4-9). "Hear, O Israel, the Lord our God, the Lord is one."

Shemini Atzereth

(Eighth Day of Assembly)

The solemn synagogue assembly which is the eighth day of the SUKKOTH festivals.

Shemittah

Cancellation of debts and soil left uncultivated in sabbatical year.

Shemoneh Esre

"Eighteen"—the number of blessings originally in the important part of the daily prayers recited in silence while worshipers stand—hence this name is applied to all such standing prayers, although the daily service now has nineteen and other services seven blessings. Combines adoration with entreaty. Also called Amidah (standing) or simply Tefillah (prayer).

Shemoth

Exodus.

Sheol

Limbo of the dead, sometimes correlated with "hell."

Shetar

Writ; legal document.

Sheva Berakhot

Seven Benedictions recited at end of wedding service.

Shevat

Fifth month of Jewish year.

Shibboleth

Gileadites recognized their enemies, the Ephraimites, by their sibillation of this word ("ear of corn"). The word is now used to mean "catchword."

Shidduch

Matrimonial match.

Shiflut

Humility (Chasidic).

Shimonowitz, David

(Kiev, 1886-1956)

In 1921 this Hebrew poet settled in Palestine; his dominant theme is life in the Holy Land, but he has written on every poetic theme, and has translated the great Russian writers into Hebrew.

Shinnui hashem

Formal changing of sick person's name, to foil the Angel of Death.

Shiur

Fixed measure; generally used to designate Talmudic study hour.

Shivah

Seven—days of mourning for close relative—parent, child, brother, sister, spouse; with specific observances.

Shlimmazel

One who is accident prone; hard-luck guy.

Shlonsky, Abraham

(Ukraine, 1900—–)

Israeli poet whose works appear in eight volumes.

Shneur, Zalman

(Russia, 1887—–)

Israeli poet and novelist, now living in U.S. Calling himself a poet of "rebellion and strife," he has to his credit a vast output of prose and verse.

Shochet

Ritual slaughterer.

Shofar

The unadorned ram's horn (the ram was sacrificed by Abraham in Isaac's place) sounded during month of Ellul, on Rosh ha-Shanah, and at conclusion of Yom Kippur, which has assumed deep traditional meaning as the holy cry for the gathering of the faithful. During Bible days, its blast announced coming of Sabbath, festival, New Moon, or other events. Also reminiscent of Jericho's fall under trumpet blasts.

Shofetim

Judges; book of the Bible.

Shoham, Mattisyahu

(Poland, 1893-1937)

Poet and dramatist in Hebrew, with Biblical and Palestinian themes.

Sholem Aleichem

(Sholem Rabinovitch, Yiddish, 1859-1916)

The tragi-comedian of Jewish literature. Folk-lore style, mingling pathos and humor. Born in Russia, left for Switzerland in 1904, came to America in 1914. Most famous works: *Menakhem Mendel, Tevye der Milkhiker, Motel dem Khazans, Funem Yarid.* Many tales dramatized for stage and films.

Shomer

Watchman, in old Palestine and modern Israel.

Shtadlan

From Aramaic "to persuade"; medieval local personage who employed his influence in behalf of his Jewish community.

Shtettel

Yiddish word for "little town."

Shul

Yiddish for synagogue and place of study, from German "*Schule*."

Shulchan Arukh

(Prepared Table)

Authoritative code of Jewish law, by Joseph Caro. Chief commentary, by Moses Isserles, is called Mappah (Tablecloth).

Shushan Purim

Day after Purim; citizens of Shushan, capital of Persia, were apprised of saving of Jews a day later.

Siddur

(Order—of prayers)

Daily prayer book. Early one prepared by SAADIA GAON (tenth century). Order differs among several groups, such as Ashkenazim, Sephardim, Italians. Many portions originate in Bible, particularly Psalms. Siddur of Amram (860); earlier collection differs greatly from the later used siddurim.

Sidra

Bible portion of the week, read on Sabbath.

Sifra, Sifre

Halakhic midrashim to Leviticus, Numbers, Deuteronomy.

Simchah

Joy.

Simchat Torah

The festival of Rejoicing in the Law, the last day of SUKKOTH festivals, with exultant dance and song, when the annual cycle of Torah reading is concluded and begun anew.

Simeon

Son of Jacob by Leah; progenitor of one of the tribes of Israel.

Simeon ben Lakish

(Resh Lakish)

Third century Palestinian amora who combined great physical strength with a noble heart and a powerful mind.

Simeon ben Shetach

Stern judge and president of SANHEDRIN first century B.C.E. He brought the Sanhedrin back under PHARISAIC control.

Simeon ben Yochai

Second-century tanna, a disciple of Akiba. Anti-Roman, he hid from them after the ill-fated BAR KOKHBA revolt; this gave rise to many legends concerning his years in a cave. A strict disciplinarian, he is remembered for his systemization of the Law, his saintliness, and (erroneously) as author of the Zohar.

Sin

Judaism rejects the doctrine of original sin. Adam and Eve suffered for their digression; every man and woman may choose the way of grace or guilt.

Singer, Israel J.

(1893-1944)

Known chiefly for his novel, *The Brothers Ashkenazi,* this Polish-born naturalistic Yiddish writer lived his final years in America. (W) *East of Eden.*

Sirach, Jesus, Son of

(About 200 B.C.)

Ever since the book written by Jesus, Son of Sirach, has become known it has edified readers of all succeeding generations up to the present day. It has confirmed pious people in their faith. It has impressed skeptical-minded readers by its vigorous conviction. It has inspired poets, philosophers, statesmen and plain people. Above all, it has been valued as a rich fountain of proverbial wisdom and the personal confession of a man of large experience. Although it has not been accepted into the Protestant canon and was placed among the books of Apocrypha, it has generally been as highly appreciated as the books of the Bible itself. The author was a contemporary of the high priest Simon II who died in 199 B.C., and he was certainly no longer alive when the Jewish people were afflicted by the persecutions which preceded the rise of the Maccabees. In his youth, Jesus ben Sirach had studied the Bible and books of popular wisdom.

Then a calumniator endangered his life and forced him to flee from his native town, but after a while he was vindicated and lived for the rest of his life in Jerusalem. During his exile, he meditated on his misfortune, and observed the vicissitudes of life which others had to endure. These experiences, and not so much his previous readings, are the substance of his book. He was neither a priest nor a *Sofer* (skilled interpreter of the law), but a layman who used to deliver popular speeches. His book was translated into Greek by his grandson under the title *Wisdom of Jesus the Son of Sirach.* Its Latin title is *Ecclesiasticus.* It also was translated into many other languages. The Hebrew original was lost. In 1896, some parts of it were found in a cellar of the Ezra Synagogue in Cairo. Later these were augmented so that now about three-fifths of the original are extant.

Sivan

Ninth month of the Jewish year.

Siyum

"Ending" of study of a sacred volume; a final discussion is held, and there is a party.

Slaves

Not prohibited in Jewish state, but completely protected. They had to be released in seven years, and fully remunerated.

Smolenskin, Perez

(1842-1885)

Known for his journalistic style in modern Hebrew, this Russian novelist and editor called on the Jews for a national revival. (W) *Am Olam, Ha-To'eh be-Darke ha-Hayim.*

Sneeze

Blessed by many—a custom prohibited by Talmud as superstitious.

Sofer

(Scribe)

Today, writer of Torah scrolls; Ezra was both copier and expounder of Holy Writ, and later soferim were a guild of authorities on text and interpretation.

Sokolow, Nahum

(Poland, 1859–London, 1936)

Man of letters and Zionist leader; created modern Hebrew journalism. (W) *History of Zionism.*

Solomon

Great ruler and personality of tenth century B.C.E., who left his stamp on Israel and the world. He organized Israel into an empire, reformed its government, sponsored voyages of discovery as far as West Africa and possibly India, and encouraged architecture whose vestiges still remain. His name betokens a lover of peace; but he also achieved wealth in material things and in wisdom. Because of his reputed knowledge of natural history, for centuries Solomon was considered ruler not only of men but of the spirits of the air and waters; he was made the founder of a mystical, magical order. Born in Jerusalem, he made it a famed religious and literary center. He has always been the symbol of a wise monarch; and many later writings were ascribed to him by the authors. However, his many foreign wives and high taxation led to the breakup of the kingdom after his death.

Soncino

Family who started printing of Talmud, Bible, and other Jewish works in Italy, 1483. Today a publisher employing that name produces great works and translations of Jewish classics.

Song of Songs

(Canticles)

Love song ascribed to Solomon, interpreted as picture of divine love for Israel.

Sotah

Woman suspected of adultery.

Spinoza, Baruch

(1632-1677)

For more than a century after Spinoza's works were published, their author was objurgated with embitterment by Catholics, Protestants, Jews and freethinkers alike. Even David Hume, in general a man of kindly disposition, branded him as "infame," and Moses Mendelssohn, the affable advocate of tolerance, was horrified and disbelieving when he heard that his friend Lessing had adopted Spinoza's doctrine. A great change was inaugurated by Herder and Goethe, who became Spinozists, and revered Spinoza as a saint. So did Heinrich Heine. Post-Kantian philosophers and Romantic poets in Germany were deeply influenced by Spinoza's conception of nature. In modern times, Spinoza is universally recognized as a philosopher of unsurpassed sublimity and profundity. Even his critics agree that Spinoza had a most lovable personality, one of the purest characters in the history of mankind. Despite his delicate feelings and the subtlety of his definitions, Spinoza's mind was unsophisticated, and regardless of the boldness of his thoughts and the sternness of his will to draw his conclusions logically and without any regard to personal inclinations, Spinoza was calm, benevolent, fond of plain people. He earned his living by grinding optical lenses and declined an appointment as professor at the University of Heidelberg because he preferred independence to honor. Spinoza belonged to a Jewish family which had been exiled from Spain and Portugal, and had finally settled in Holland. Before studying Latin, the natural sciences, and the philosophy of Hobbes and Descartes, he had studied the Hebrew Bible, the Talmud, medieval Jewish literature, and probably Cabbalah. In 1656, he was put under the ban by the Jewish community of Amsterdam because of his opposition to traditional doctrines of Judaism, including those that were also sacred tenets of Christianity. Detached from the Jewish community, Spinoza manifested indifference to Jews and Judaism. With his investigation of the sacred Scriptures he gave an impetus to modern Biblical criticism. But the elements of his Jewish education, especially his acquaintance with medieval Jewish philosophy, remain visible in his conception of the oneness of God and in his personal piety. Spinoza's chief work is entitled *Ethics.* It could have been named "Metaphysics" with equal justice, for Spinoza was thoroughly convinced that the knowledge of the ultimate reality involves the norm of human action and implies the measure of personal perfection. Philosophical thinking was, to Spinoza, self-education and improvement of the mind of the thinker. His aim was to obtain, by means of reason and science, the same trust in rules of human behavior that religious traditions claimed to grant their believers. Contrary to Descartes, he denied the possibility of harmonizing reason with Biblical revelation, and, in that way, Spinoza, not Descartes, became the symbol of the end of medieval philosophy. The scientific method offered to Spinoza not only the measure of moral evaluation but a means of gaining eternal bliss. To win supreme happiness or "unceasing joy," Spinoza said, man has to attain knowledge of his union with the whole of nature. All individual beings, whatever is popularly supposed to be a real thing, are regarded by Spinoza as mere modifications of but one infinite substance which has an infinite number of attributes, of which, however, only two, namely thought and extension, are perceptible by man. This one substance which is in itself and conceived through itself alone, is the only object of true knowledge, and is identical with God whose will is identical with the laws of nature. He who knows nature knows God. Increasing knowledge of nature means increasing love of God. From this proposition of the oneness and universality of God, Spinoza has deduced *more geometrico,* in a manner following the example of geometrical demonstrations, his definitions of all particular objects in the realms of extension and thought. He finally arrived at his much admired description of the intellectual love of God which is characterized as an absolutely disinterested feeling, the humble cognizance of all-governing necessity and at the same time the complete liberation of the soul from disturbing passions. Neither to laud nor to blame but to understand is the principle of Spinoza's attitude toward life. (W) *The Ethics, The Improvement of the Understanding, Political Tractate, The Book of God, The Theologico-Political Tractate, Hebrew Grammar.*

Sprinzak, Joseph

Speaker of the Israel Knesset.

Streimel

Broad-brimmed fur hat traditionally worn in parts of Eastern Europe.

Sukkah

(Hut)

Temporary dwelling, with open sky showing, reminiscent of Israel's wanderings in the desert. Once also slept in, it is now used for meals during the festival of SUKKOTH. It is decorated with twigs, straw, fruits, and vegetables.

Sukkoth

Feasts of Booths, or Ingathering; fall harvest festival.

Sunday School

Some Jewish groups offer only Sunday morning instruction to Jewish children, as is the case with most Protestant sects; but even the most extreme among rabbis and lay readers consider this limited training insufficient for proper appreciation and understanding of their faith.

Sunday services

Introduced, to replace Sabbath worship by Reform congregation in Germany, 1845; and in Baltimore, 1854. Now largely discontinued, with a return to Sabbath and Sabbath eve services.

Sura

City in Babylonia; seat of Talmudic academy.

Synagogue

Greek, "lead together"; Jewish house of worship, or Bet ha-Knesset.

Synagogue, The Great

(Knesset ha-Gedolah)

The Great Assembly, predecessor to the SANHEDRIN and GERUSIA during the pre-Maccabean Second Commonwealth. The dominant legislative body of from 85 to 120 men, tracing its tradition to Moses and playing a determining part in establishing the canon, ritual and ceremonial for ensuing ages. It was also called in times of national emergency and exercised a curbing influence upon the priestly sect.

Syndic

Official of the Jewish community council.

Synod of Usha

(c. 135)

A dramatically called assembly of the Talmudic teachers after the Hadrianic persecutions with the purpose of re-establishing normal religious life. Under the leadership of Simeon ben Gamaliel ha-Nasi it reopened religious schools and activated the Temple services.

Szold, Henrietta

(Baltimore, 1860—Jerusalem, 1945)

American-born editor, translator, women's leader, founder of Hadassah, who died in Jerusalem while conducting social work in behalf of young migrants to Palestine.

Szyk, Arthur

(1894-1956)

Polish-American miniaturist, book designer, illustrator; many awards and exhibitions.

T

Taanit

Fast, fast day; tractate of Talmud.

Tabernacle

(*Ohel Moed*)

The sanctuary on wheels borne by the Israelites in their wanderings, containing the Ark of the Covenant. Its last station after the occupation of Canaan was at Shiloh. Only the high priest could enter its Holy of Holies.

Tabernacles, Feast of

See SUKKOTH.

Tachlit

(Purpose)

Material or practical end result of a planned action.

Taharah

Cleansing; the word is applied to traditional ways of cleaning and clothing a corpse.

Takkanah

(Improvement)

Special supplementary ordinance designated to strengthen observance of Jewish law and morals.

Takhrikhim

Shrouds prescribed by Jewish law.

Tal

(Dew)

The prayer for dew (in Palestine) recited on first day of Passover.

Tallith

Prayer shawl. Of wool, silk, or other fabric, bearing fringes (tzitzit) on each of its four corners. There is a tallith katan (little prayer shawl) worn over undershirt by many pious Jews. (Num. 15:37-41; Deut. 22:12.)

Talmid Chakham

Student of true knowledge as interpreted by the Talmudic sages.

Talmud

The Talmud, which may be rendered from the Hebrew as "Research," is one of the world's ten great works of divinely inspired literature. Like the Koran and other post-Judean books of holy nature, it is impossible to conceive of the Talmud without the Torah, the ancient Books of Moses. In fact, the Talmud is the Torah perpetuated. As long as the great Solomonic Temple towered over the lands along the Jordan, the rituals, ceremonies and observances, sacrifices, commands and prohibitions made the Torah a living spirit in Israel. It was both state law and religious fountain head, the guide to daily conduct and the basis of family and social structure for all the adherents of the Covenant. But with the sudden advent of the overbearing and hostile Caesarian Empire, the sacred walls of the Temple crumbled under the Roman ram and the people of Palestine were scattered to the four corners of the world, to become the most remarkable wandering people of all time. Thrust into strange lands with alien customs to which they were forced to adjust their own deeply felt faith, the dispersed Hebrews were often and in many places bewildered as to how to abide by the laws of the Torah, the Covenant they had made with their Lord. A thousand practical problems arose before the Jews of the First Century of the Common Era: problems concerning marriage and divorce and other aspects of family life; concerning personal hygiene and ritual purity; concerning civil and ceremonial law, dietary obligations and sacrificial cults; concerning the observance of holidays and festivals, the keeping of the Sabbath, the treatment of illness, the care of the poor, and so on. For a hundred years and more, distinguished scholars labored to formulate a new set of laws which would reinterpret the ancient Mosaic concepts to the sons of Israel living in a pagan world. Finally, in third-century Palestine, under the editorship of Rabbi Judah, called "The Prince," all the new writings of Biblical interpretation were correlated into a volume of six books known as the Mishnah, or "Repetition." This became the core of the Talmud. During the next three hundred years the Mishnah was supplemented by many recorded discussions or commentaries, contributed by Babylonian as well as Palestinian rabbis. Some of these were legalistic, some philosophic, some folklorist, some allegorical. These later writings, known as the *Gemara,* or "Learning," were intended to expound the Mishnah and to facilitate the understanding of its difficult passages. Thus for almost five hundred years the great *hakhamin,* or sages, of Babylon, Jerusalem and other academic centers worked in setting down first the Mishnah and then the Gemara, which together constitute the Talmud. By the sixth century the compilation of the Talmud had come to an end, but the commentaries and addenda have never ceased, even up to our own days. In the Middle Ages, the philosopher Maimonides, the commentator Rashi, and the codifier Caro were among those who brought about a renaissance of Talmudic study in Western Europe. Many sayings and parables from such Talmudic scribes as Hillel and others became proverbial in the non-Jewish world also. The books of the Talmud are uneven. They range from severe theological legalism to unsurpassed beauty of legendary literature. To borrow a phrase from one of our masters, "Who would forgo a walk through the forest because some of the trees are dry and barren?"

Talmud Torah

Elementary Hebrew school.

Tamchui

Charity plate.

Tamid

Daily Temple sacrifice.

Tammuz

Tenth month of the Jewish year.

Tanchuma

Fourth-century collection of homiletic and Haggadic literature.

Tanna

(Teacher)

The earlier Talmudic scholars, mentioned in the Mishnah (primary sections of the Talmud) and the Baraitot, apocryphal Mishnah.

Targum

(Translation)

Traditionally the name given the Aramaic translation of the Bible, read to the populace in Babylonian periods. The custom of reading services in Aramaic following the Hebrew goes back to hundreds of years before the great diaspora. Except for some interpolations and paraphrases, the Targum Bavli, also known as the Targum Onkeles, is a very faithful translation. Less faithful to the text are the Targum Yerushalmi and others of fragmentary character.

Tarphon

Second century tanna whose school was located at Lydda.

Taryag

The letters of this word in Hebrew add up to 613, all the precepts (mitzvot) of the Torah.

Tashlikh

(Casting)

Custom of casting off sins, symbolically, in running stream, on Rosh ha-Shanah: "Thou shalt cast thy sins into the depths of the sea."

Technion

The Israel Institute of Technology at Haifa.

Tefillah

(Prayer)
See SHEMONEH ESRE.

Tefillin

(Phylacteries)

The leather cubes strapped to arms and head by observant Jews during daily morning prayers; each contains quotations from the Bible.

Tehillim

Psalms.

Tel Aviv

Hill of Spring; name of Israel's largest city, from Herzl's utopian narrative.

Templo

Actual name, Jacob Judah Leon (1603-1675, Amsterdam). Scholar known for drawing reconstructed Temple.

Ten Commandments

See DECALOGUE.

Tenach

Trilogy of Torah, Prophets, and Writings (Hagiographa), formed from initial letters of the Hebrew Torah, Neviim, Ketuvim.

Terach

Father of Abraham, who smashed his father's idols.

Terefah

Food not ritually permitted; from Hebrew meaning "torn" —i.e., an animal improperly slaughtered.

Territorialism

Movement instituted by Israel Zangwill to substitute another home, such as African Uganda, for Palestine, as a refuge for the world's Jews.

Terumah

Removal; heave-offering; tithe for priests.

Teshuvah

Repentance.

Tetragrammaton

(Greek, "Sign of the Four"—JHVH)

First used by Philo as symbol for the "Nameless One," identical with the tannaitic Shem ha-Meforash. The word Yahweh was pronounced only by the High Priest, on Yom Kippur. The Tetragrammaton played a significant part in numerological speculations of cabbalistic mysticism.

Teveth

Fourth month of the Jewish year.

Thirty-six Righteous

(Tzaddikim)

See LAMED-VAV TZADDIKIM.

Tiberias

City on Sea of Galilee in which Herod and successors dwelt; later, scene of last Great Sanhedrin.

Tikkun

(Lel Shavuoth ve-Hoshanah Rabbah)

An anthology of Biblical and post-Biblical literature read on the nights of Shavuoth and Hoshanah Rabbah; this pious study is calculated to gain God's favor for the students and worshipers.

Tishah B'Av

The ninth day of the month Av, on which both Temples were destroyed and other calamities came upon Israel; a fast day.

Tishri

First month of Jewish year.

Tiyyul

Promenade; hike; migration.

Todah

Thank offering in the Temple.

Tohu va-Vohu

"Unformed and void"—state of the earth at creation; chaos.

Tokhechah

Sermon of curses, recounting punishment for sinning; cf. Lev. 26; Deut. 28.

Toledoth Jeshu

History of Jesus; Hebrew legends popular in Middle Ages.

Tolerance

Cardinal precept of the Jewish faith; the Jews have rarely made any effort to proselytize. ("The righteous of all Nations are worthy of immortality.")

Torah

Torah means, in the literal Hebrew, *instruction,* or *guidance,* and is used in this sense by the ancient prophets and sages. Prior to the first destruction of the great Temple in Jerusalem, by "Torah" the Hebrews meant the Books attributed to Moses. Shortly after the time of the Second Temple, the final settlement of the Canon was made at Jamnia about 100 C.E. leading to the Bible's present form as codified by the seventh century rabbis known as Masoretes. Therefore, the Hebrew Bible *in toto,* as well as all Talmudic and later literature was often referred to as Torah. The Hebrew Bible as it appears in our texts today is an anthology of thirty-nine books, reckoned as twenty-two, written for the most part in Hebrew, a little of it in Aramaic. (The uncanonized apocryphal sections are in Greek as well as Hebrew.) There is hardly any doubt that these books were written over a time stretching more than a thousand years. A much larger segment than commonly supposed is written in poetic and aphoristic form. In this sense the Torah is to be considered one of the world's greatest collections of pure literature. Basically it contains five types of material: (1) the legendary tales, frequently influencing faraway Asian story writers, as in India and Persia; (2) the historical books (of remarkable accuracy, as shown by recent archaeological findings); (3) the ritualistic codes with their 613 commandments and prohibitions as to diet, habitat, marriage, prayer service, sacrifices, and legal procedure; (4) the prophetic sermons on current political and social issues; (5) the philosophical and poetical works. Is, anywhere, or was at any time, another volume of writings such as this, whose impact set aflame the lands between the Nile and the Euphrates more than three thousand years ago—a flame that has never ceased to burn all these millennia and has leapt from continent to continent, from tongue to tongue, from heart to heart. Show me a village of people and I will find somewhere among them a trace of the Mosaic flame, be it in a book, a house of worship, a painting, a sculptured figurine, a phrase of music, or the memory of a sage proverb from Solomon, the king of kings. And even in places where the Torah has been defiled and its people erased, you will find the ashes of Israel still glimmering to remind the forgetful. The Torah cannot be forgotten nor can it be thrown aside. If one had such intent, he would have to rip out a thousand statues and portraits from a thousand walls, and a thousand temples and churches from land to land. For millennia the people of the East and the West have grown and flourished in the breath of the Torah. The songs of its inspired sages reverberated in the poets, the dramatists, the painters, the sculptors, the fabulists, the preachers, the statesmen, the legislators, the philosophers, and the people at large, forever seeking justice. If there ever was a book that has moved the world, this is it. It was of this Torah that Jesus said, "I come to fulfill it, not to destroy it." And it was because of the Torah that Mohammed called the Hebrews the People of the Book. The Hebrew Bible is for the most part a wreath of poetry and aphoristic rhythm. Except for the historic-prophetic and ritualistic citations, this book consists, most significantly, of poems and aphorisms of the two kings, David and his son Solomon. So much has been written on the subject of the authorship of the various Biblical books that I certainly do not wish to add to the already existing commentaries. There is no doubt that the majesty of Moses appears in many a page attributed to him, as does the wisdom of King Solomon in the writings named after him, and the incomparable poetry of his father in the Psalms. Little difference would it make today if these three greatest of the children of Jacob were princes in the palace, as in truth they were, or shepherds on a hill. The Lord showed His face to none of them, but if ever man's soul spoke His word, they did. Jew, gentile, even pagan, can listen to His word without professing religion or ritual and traditional ties. The Torah shuns neither the believing nor the faithless, be it written in the Hebrew or the vernacular. While the traditional revelations of God in the books known as Holy Writ have been transmitted to us in Hebrew, His word can be heard in any language. And if this present offering of poetry and philosophy reaches someone who could not hurdle the obstacles of a foreign tongue or foreign-seeming rituals, the purpose of this volume will have been fulfilled. As our sages have said, the ways to our Lord are wondersome, and who knows which is the better one?

Torquemada, Tomas de

See INQUISITION.

Torture

Prohibited by Jewish law. Confession was not accepted as evidence.

Tosafot

Additional commentaries and expositions of Talmudic text, appearing on pages of the Talmud on border opposite Rashi's commentary. The Baale Tosafot, so-called, were the school that flourished in France and Germany, twelfth and thirteenth centuries, with Jacob ben Meir (Rabbenu Tam) as chief master.

Tosefta

(Supplement)

Anthology of tannaitic text, parallel to Mishnah, but outside Mishnaic canon, and more expansive. Rabbi Nehemiah, second century, began the work; in the third century it was continued by Hiyya ben Abba and Oshaiah.

Touro, Judah

(1775-1854)

American merchant and philanthropist who helped build Bunker Hill Monument.

Touro Synagogue

In Newport, R.I. Oldest house of worship of American Jewry.

Trendel

Four-sided top spun by children on Chanukah; its characters are the initials of *Nes Gadol Hayah Sham*—"A great miracle took place there."

Trumpeldor, Joseph

(1882-1920)

First Jewish officer in Russian army, he became a pioneer (chalutz) in Israel, and was treacherously slain by Arabs at Tel Hai. Associated with Jabotinsky.

Tschernichovsky, Saul

(Russia, 1875–Jerusalem, 1943)

Outstanding modern Hebrew poet and fictionist, who also translated many classics in other tongues. (W) *Lenohah pessel Apollo, Hezyonat Umanginoth, Shirim, Shirim Hadoshim, Sippurim, Sefer Ha'idilliyot.*

Tur; Turim

Row, rows; used in *Arbaah Turim,* four legal code volumes by Jacob ben Asher (1269, Germany—1343, Spain).

Tzaddik

("Righteous")

Chasidic sages were so called; they were often raised by their followers to the status of direct intermediaries with God, superhuman miracle workers.

Tzedakah

Righteousness; charity.

Tzedakah box

Since charity is a basic principle of Jewish life, charity boxes are to be found in synagogues, homes, and other places where Jews gather.

Tze-enah u-Re'enah

Yiddish version of Torah for women, which appeared from fifteenth to seventeenth centuries.

Tzelem

Cross; ikon.

Tzeniut

Modesty; virtue.

Tzibbur

Congregation.

Tzitzit

Fringes, once blue and white, now all white, made with prescribed numbers of loops and knots, on the four corners of the tallith or arba kanfot ("four corners" or tallith ketanah—little prayer shawl), to be worn by Biblical command as reminder of God's ordinances.

U

Union of American Hebrew Congregations

Reform group organized by Isaac M. Wise in 1873. National organization of liberal American congregations.

Union of Orthodox Jewish Congregations of America

1,000 traditional synagogues in the U.S. and Canada.

United Synagogue of America

Union of Conservative congregations; allied group, National Women's League, and other cultural and youth groups.

Ur

City and region in Mesopotamia, birthplace of the patriarch Abraham.

Urim and Tummim

Oracular attachments to the high priest's breastplate. The words are variously translated—"revelation and truth" or "those whose words give light, and are fulfilled." Fell into disuse in post-Solomonic times.

Ussischkin, Menachem Mendel

(1863-1943)

Russian Zionist leader who became world leader of the movement, and fought partition of Palestine.

V

Vaad Leumi

First self-governing body of Jews in Palestine, elected 1931.

Vatik

Conscientiously pious man of "ancient" days.

Vayikra

Leviticus.

Veil

The custom of bridal veil goes back to Rebecca, who covered her face when meeting Isaac.

Viddui

Confession of sins, at proper times and on deathbed.

Vikkuach

Disputation: applied to compulsory medieval debates between Jews and Christians. There were many of these, the most important being Nachmanides vs. the renegade Pablo Christiani (1263).

Vital, Chaim

(Safed, 1543–Damascus, 1620)

Cabbalist; disciple and perpetuator of teachings of Isaac Luria, embodied in his work *Etz Hayyim.*

Vows

Ordinarily adhered to, but may be annulled by head of family when hurtful. They need not be maintained when made under pressure and persecution; hence the recitation of Kol Nidre (All Vows) on eve of Atonement Day.

W

Wachtnacht

Watch night; night before a circumcision, devoted to solemnity and prayer, by family, godfather, mohel, among the rigidly Orthodox.

Wailing Wall

Remaining part of Temple structure, long used for prayer and entreaty by pious Jews. Now in possession of Jordan.

Wandering Jew

Fictional character said to have taunted Jesus and been doomed to eternal wandering; he was called Ahasuerus.

Water Festival

On the second night of Sukkoth, during time of Second Temple, water was scooped from Siloam spring near Jerusalem, with torch parades, sacrifices, and dances; thus was the importance of water in the land's economy celebrated.

Weeks, Feast of

See SHAVUOTH.

Weizmann, Chaim

(1874-1952)

First president of Israel. Leading negotiator with Britain for the Balfour Declaration. Elected president of World Zionist Organization, 1920. Helped create Hebrew University.

Well poisoning

A common slander against

medieval Jews, resulting in destruction of hundreds of Jewish communities in fourteenth-century Europe.

Wig

(Sheitel)

Medieval custom, now largely abandoned, of pious Jewesses shaving their heads on marriage and covering their pates with a false piece.

Wise, Isaac Mayer

(1819-1900)

Chief factor in development of Reform Judaism in America, he immigrated from Bohemia in 1846; organized Union of American Hebrew Congregations in 1873, Hebrew Union College 1875, and Central Conference of American Rabbis 1889. Prepared first Reform prayer book, *Minhag America,* wrote *Judaism: Its Doctrines and Duties, The Essence of Judaism,* and many other works.

Wise, Stephen S.

(Budapest, 1874—New York, 1949)

Hungarian-born religious leader who founded the Free Synagogue, the Jewish Institute of Religion, and other important American Jewish Institutions.

WIZO

(Women's International Zionist Organization)

Equivalent to the Hadassah Organization outside the U.S. This international group provides economic, educational, and health assistance to Israel.

Wolffsohn, David

(Russia, 1856—Hamburg, 1914)

Zionist leader, successor to Herzl, founder of Jewish Colonial Trust.

Women

Traditional law requires separation of women from men at worship; they are exempt from prayer quorum (minyan), or serving as witnesses in ritual matters. Reform Judaism gives women full equality in all religious matters.

Women's gallery

Separate section for women at synagogue services, not observed by conservative and liberal Jews.

Workmen's Circle

National fraternal and self-help organization, of socialist leanings.

World of Emanation

Highest of the four cabbalistic worlds between the Infinite and our mundane sphere.

World Jewish Congress

Established in Geneva 1936, to protect the rights of Jews everywhere.

Wouk, Herman

(1915—)

Distinguished American novelist and dramatist; Orthodox Jew, visiting professor at Yeshiva University. Among his works are *The Caine Mutiny* and *Marjorie Morningstar.*

Y

Yaari, Judah

(Galicia, 1900—)
Israeli novelist.

Yad

(Hand)
Pointer, generally metal, with hand-shaped end, to guide reading of Torah scroll.

Yaknehaz

Word formed from initials of names of five benedictions for evening kiddush of a festival beginning Sunday. Confused with German words for "He chases the hare"—hence certain illustrations in Passover Haggadah.

Yalkut Shimeoni

Haggadic anthology of midrashim on all the Bible, many of which early works have been lost. Middle Ages; of uncertain authorship.

Yamim Noraim

Days of Awe, comprising Rosh ha-Shanah and Yom Kippur.

Yarmulke

Skullcap worn by observant Jews.

Yashar, Sefer ha-

Book of the Righteous; popular retelling of Biblical events from Adam to Joshua, probably written in Spain, twelfth century.

Yavam

Husband's brother, or *levir*, upon whom devolved the duty of marrying the former's widow, if left without issue.

Yebamah

Under Biblical laws, childless widow who was commanded to marry late husband's brother, so that a child might be named after the departed. Could be released by ceremony of chalitzah.

Yehoash

(Russia, 1871–Chicago, 1927)

Real name Solomon Bloomgarden; poet, novelist, translator, lexicographer; rendered Bible into classic Yiddish. (W) *The Feet of the Messenger.*

Yerach

Month, moon.

Yere-Shamayim

One who fears the Lord.

Yeshivah

(Seat)

Talmudic school of higher education.

Yeshivah-bachur

Talmud student.

Yetzer Ha-ra

The "evil desire" inherent in every human.

Yetzer Tov

Good inclination.

YHVH

Tetragram of the Lord's name; not to be spoken. Commonly substituted by Adonai (Lord, Eternal).

Yibbum

Marrying the wife of a brother who has died without issue.

Yichus

Pedigree.

Yiddish

Language widely spoken and

written by Jews, a carry-over of Middle High German, incorporating some Hebrew words and local idioms (Polish, Russian, Ukrainian, Rumanian, English, and others). Hebrew print and script used, with special values. Verbs of Hebrew origin are Germanized; nouns of German origin, Hebraized. Gigantic literature, with such authors as Mendele Mocher Sefarim, Sholem Aleichem, I. L. Peretz, Mordecai Spector, Morris Rosenfeld, Solomon An-ski, Sholem Asch, David Pinski, Abraham Reisin, Jacob Gordin. Original chief center of Yiddish was in Russia, where now USSR discourages its use.

Yigdal

Poetic adaptation of the thirteen articles of faith by Maimonides, recited at beginning or end of services.

Yirat Chet

Fear of sin.

Yirat Shamayim

Fear of Heaven.

Yishuv

Settlement; applied to modern population of Israel.

Yizkor

("May He remember")

Prayers for the departed, recited on Yom Kippur, Shemini Atzereth, last day of Passover, second day of Shavuoth.

Yom Kippur

See ATONEMENT, DAY OF.

Yom Tov

(Good Day)

Holiday or festival.

Young Judea

American Zionist children and youth group.

Young Men's and Young Women's Hebrew Associations

Social and cultural activities in large American cities, with emphasis on Jewish elements.

Yovel

Year of Jubilee.

Z

Zacuto, Moses

(Amsterdam, 1625–Mantua, 1697)

Writer on Cabbalah, law; liturgical poems, commentaries.

Zaddik

See TZADDIK.

Zangwill, Israel

(England, 1864-1926)

Outstanding novelist, essayist, and playwright, largely on Jewish themes; opposed assimilationism; supported Zionism (and territorialism). Among his books: *Children of the Ghetto, Dreamers of the Ghetto, King of Schnorrers, The Voice of Jerusalem, The Melting Pot.*

Zebulun

One of the sons of Jacob; one of the tribes descended from him.

Zechariah

One of the minor prophets to whom is attributed the collection of prophecies and apocalyptic visions constituting the book bearing his name.

Zedekiah

Last king of Judah when the land was conquered by Nebuchadnezzar and the people were taken to Babylonian exile, 586 B.C.E.

Zekenim

Elders; term first applied to successors of Joshua.

Zemanim

Organ of the Progressive party in Israel.

Zemirot

Songs made part of Sabbath and other meals; devotional.

Zephaniah

Prophet of time when all nations will join in obedience to the Lord.

Zerubbabel

He brought first group of exiles back from Persia 537 B.C.E., and instituted measures for reconstituting the land and Temple of Israel.

Zhitlovsky, Chaim

(1865-1943)

Philosopher of Yiddishism and Russian Socialism.

Zimmun

Designation for a purpose; court summons; three or more common diners, required for saying of grace.

Zion

Jerusalem hill on which stood tower of David; used today to mean all Jerusalem, all Israel.

Zionides

Hymns mourning loss of Zion by Judah Halevi.

Zionism

Movement to re-establish State of Israel. Term used in 1886 by Nathan Birnbaum. Always in Jewish thought and prayer; foreseen by Spinoza; directly initiated by Viennese journalist, Theodor Herzl, who had reported the infamous Dreyfus trial in Paris. Herzl wrote *The Jewish State*, as the sole means of freeing the Jewish people of constant humiliation and persecution by their Christian hosts. As a political movement, culminated in the establishment of the Jewish State in 1948.

Zionist Organization of America

Oldest and most powerful nationalist Jewish group.

Zohar

Basic work of Cabbalah, mystical Aramaic commentary on the Book of Moses, ascribed to Simeon ben Johai of second century, but probably written by Moses de Leon, of the thirteenth.

Zugot

Pairs. Collective name of head and assistant head of SANHEDRIN before Hillel.

Zunz, Leopold

(1794-1886)

Pathfinder of the Science of Judaism; historian of Jewish literature; protagonist of liberalism and harmonization of Judaism with modern thought; defended vernacular in synagogue sermons in *Sermons of the Jews* and reform of ritual and practice. Opposed monotonous singsong of traditional service and sale of honors. Also favored vernacular for those ignorant of Hebrew prayers, organ and hymnal music with mixed choir, abbreviated worship, and fuller religious rights for women.